T0301899

An Analysis of

Jane Jacobs's

The Death and Life of
Great American Cities

Martin Fuller
with
Ryan Moore

Published by Macat International Ltd
24:13 Coda Centre, 189 Munster Road, London SW6 6AW.

Distributed exclusively by Routledge
2 Park Square, Milton Park, Abingdon, Oxon OX14 4RN
711 Third Avenue, New York, NY 10017, USA

Routledge is an imprint of the Taylor & Francis Group, an informa business

www.macat.com
info@macat.com

Cataloguing in Publication Data
A catalogue record for this book is available from the British Library.
Library of Congress Cataloguing-in-Publication Data is available upon request.
Cover illustration: A. Richard Allen

ISBN 978-1-912303-78-6 (hardback)
ISBN 978-1-912128-59-4 (paperback)
ISBN 978-1-912282-66-1 (e-book)

CONTENTS

THE MACAT LIBRARY

The Macat Library is a series of unique academic explorations of seminal works in the humanities and social sciences – books and papers that have had a significant and widely recognised impact on their disciplines. It has been created to serve as much more than just a summary of what lies between the covers of a great book. It illuminates and explores the influences on, ideas of, and impact of that book. Our goal is to offer a learning resource that encourages critical thinking and fosters a better, deeper understanding of important ideas.

Each publication is divided into three Sections: Influences, Ideas, and Impact. Each Section has four Modules. These explore every important facet of the work, and the responses to it.

This Section-Module structure makes a Macat Library book easy to use, but it has another important feature. Because each Macat book is written to the same format, it is possible (and encouraged!) to cross-reference multiple Macat books along the same lines of inquiry or research. This allows the reader to open up interesting interdisciplinary pathways.

To further aid your reading, lists of glossary terms and people mentioned are included at the end of this book (these are indicated by an asterisk [*] throughout) – as well as a list of works cited.

Macat has worked with the University of Cambridge to identify the elements of critical thinking and understand the ways in which six different skills combine to enable effective thinking.
Three allow us to fully understand a problem; three more give us the tools to solve it. Together, these six skills make up the **PACIER** model of critical thinking. They are:

ANALYSIS – understanding how an argument is built
EVALUATION – exploring the strengths and weaknesses of an argument
INTERPRETATION – understanding issues of meaning

CREATIVE THINKING – coming up with new ideas and fresh connections
PROBLEM-SOLVING – producing strong solutions
REASONING – creating strong arguments

To find out more, visit **WWW.MACAT.COM.**

CRITICAL THINKING AND *THE DEATH AND LIFE OF GREAT AMERICAN CITIES*

Primary critical thinking skill: EVALUATION
Secondary critical thinking skill: REASONING

Despite having no formal training in urban planning, Jane Jacobs deftly explores the strengths and weaknesses of policy arguments put forward by American urban planners in the era after World War II. They believed that the efficient movement of cars was of more value in the development of US cities than the everyday lives of the people living there.

By carefully examining their relevance in her 1961 book, *The Death and Life of Great American Cities,* Jacobs dismantles these arguments by highlighting their shortsightedness. She evaluates the information to hand and comes to a very different conclusion, that urban planners ruin great cities, because they don't understand that it is a city's social interaction that makes it great. Proposals and policies that are drawn from planning theory do not consider the social dynamics of city life. They are in thrall to futuristic fantasies of a modern way of living that bears no relation to reality, or to the desires of real people living in real spaces. Professionals lobby for separation and standardization, splitting commercial, residential, industrial, and cultural spaces. However, a truly visionary approach to urban planning should incorporate spaces with mixed uses, together with short, walkable blocks, large concentrations of people, and a mix of new and old buildings. This creates true urban vitality.

ABOUT THE AUTHOR OF THE ORIGINAL WORK

American author, journalist, and activist **Jane Jacobs** was born Jane Butzner in 1916 in Scranton, Pennsylvania. She moved to New York City in 1934, where she became a journalist, writing for magazines including Architectural Forum and Fortune. As a resident of Lower Manhattan's Greenwich Village, she joined a grassroots movement in the late 1950s to save her neighborhood from its planned destruction to make way for new expressways. Jacobs expressed her opposition to dominant yet ill-conceived ideas of city planning and policy in her 1961 work *The Death and Life of Great American Cities.* Many urban planners have since adopted its ideas to make cities more diverse, walkable, and densely concentrated. Jacobs died in 2006 at the age of 89.

ABOUT THE AUTHORS OF THE ANALYSIS

Dr Martin Fuller holds a PhD in sociology from the University of Cambridge, focusing on the sociology of art in New York and Berlin. He is currently a researcher at the Technische Universität, Berlin.

Dr Ryan Moore holds PhDs in sociology and cultural analysis from the University of California, San Diego. He has taught at universities across America and is the author of *Sells Like Teen Spirit: Music, Youth Culture, and Social Crisis* (New York: NYU Press, 2009).

ABOUT MACAT

GREAT WORKS FOR CRITICAL THINKING

Macat is focused on making the ideas of the world's great thinkers accessible and comprehensible to everybody, everywhere, in ways that promote the development of enhanced critical thinking skills.

It works with leading academics from the world's top universities to produce new analyses that focus on the ideas and the impact of the most influential works ever written across a wide variety of academic disciplines. Each of the works that sit at the heart of its growing library is an enduring example of great thinking. But by setting them in context – and looking at the influences that shaped their authors, as well as the responses they provoked – Macat encourages readers to look at these classics and game-changers with fresh eyes. Readers learn to think, engage and challenge their ideas, rather than simply accepting them.

'Macat offers an amazing first-of-its-kind tool for interdisciplinary learning and research. Its focus on works that transformed their disciplines and its rigorous approach, drawing on the world's leading experts and educational institutions, opens up a world-class education to anyone.'

Andreas Schleicher
Director for Education and Skills, Organisation for Economic Co-operation and Development

'Macat is taking on some of the major challenges in university education … They have drawn together a strong team of active academics who are producing teaching materials that are novel in the breadth of their approach.'

Prof Lord Broers,
former Vice-Chancellor of the University of Cambridge

'The Macat vision is exceptionally exciting. It focuses upon new modes of learning which analyse and explain seminal texts which have profoundly influenced world thinking and so social and economic development. It promotes the kind of critical thinking which is essential for any society and economy.
This is the learning of the future.'

Rt Hon Charles Clarke, former UK Secretary of State for Education

'The Macat analyses provide immediate access to the critical conversation surrounding the books that have shaped their respective discipline, which will make them an invaluable resource to all of those, students and teachers, working in the field.'

Professor William Tronzo, University of California at San Diego

WAYS IN TO THE TEXT

KEY POINTS

- Jane Jacobs (1916–2006) was a US journalist who criticized urban renewal*—the policy of reconstructing cities, frequently by demolishing neighborhoods for the construction of automotive highways—and postwar city planning.

- *The Death and Life of Great of American Cities* exposed the failures of urban planning* (the process of designing cities with concerns for infrastructure, transportation, communications, and public welfare).

- Jacobs presented an alternative method for understanding cities based on the firsthand observation of social interaction. She proposed ways to make cities more diverse, walkable, and densely concentrated.

Who Was Jane Jacobs?

Jane Jacobs, the author of *The Death and Life of Great of American Cities* (1961), was born in 1916 in Scranton, Pennsylvania. She moved to New York City in 1934 to become a journalist, writing for the journal *Architectural Forum** and other magazines. In the late 1950s, Jacobs helped lead a movement to save Lower Manhattan—the southern part of New York City's largest island, with neighborhoods such as East Village and Chinatown, as well as the World Trade Center—from "urban renewal."[1] This eventually stopped plans that would have destroyed several neighborhoods in order to construct new roads. She published *The Death and Life of Great American Cities* in 1961, and its criticism of urban planning made an immediate impact by exposing the failures of urban renewal after World War II.* Many urban planners have since adopted Jacobs's ideas for making cities more diverse, walkable, and densely concentrated.

Jacobs moved to Toronto in 1968, where she joined a local movement opposed to the Spadina Expressway,* an urban renewal project that would have demolished numerous homes, parks, and small businesses.[2] Just as in New York City, this local movement succeeded in canceling the expressway's construction. Jacobs lived in Toronto for the rest of her life, and wrote six more books before her death in 2006, mainly about cities and economics. In the 1970s she became an advocate for the independence of Canada's French-speaking region of Quebec, publishing a book about the issue of Quebec separatism in 1980. However, *Death and Life* continues to be her most influential work.

What Does *Death and Life* Say?

Death and Life challenged dominant ideas of city planning and policy. Jacobs argues that urban planners destroy great cities because they do not consider how people live in them, and offers alternative ideas about how cities work developed by observing interactions in the streets. She insists that diversity, concentration, and mixture make cities great. In contrast, separation and standardization were the central principles of urban planning. Whereas planners assumed density and diversity created chaos, Jacobs sees these as sources of order and safety.

Ignoring the dynamics of city life, planners concocted proposals from urban theory. Jacobs sees these as fantasies that promised a better way of life but in reality accelerated deprivation and decline—without considering how millions of people actually inhabit and interact in urban spaces. Jacobs insists that these interactions characterize the life of the city. Urban planning could only succeed when its proposals took these social dynamics into account.

When she wrote *Death and Life*, Jacobs lived in in New York City's Greenwich Village,* a characterful neighborhood in Lower Manhattan, where her analysis was shaped by her observations of people and their social interactions. Jacobs also teamed up with other residents to save their neighborhoods from urban renewal projects. New York's "master builder" Robert Moses* planned to build an expressway through Manhattan. However, Jacobs and her neighbors rallied to stop Moses' plan. Their struggle was urgent because the expressway would have led to the demolition of numerous neighborhoods. Jacobs's fight against urban renewal was not just intellectual—it was political and personal. Moses' proposal would have impacted Jacobs because she lived in Greenwich Village, a neighborhood Moses condemned as a "slum," but that today is a hub for New York music, arts, and culture.

Death and Life offers several suggestions for urban planning alternatives. Jacobs outlined four conditions to create diversity in any city:

- First, a district should support a mixture of uses. While urban planners segregated commercial, residential, industrial, and cultural spaces, Jacobs maintained that city life improved when these different functions mixed.
- Second, blocks of streets must be as short as possible to make them easier to walk and promote interaction.
- Third, districts should include a mix of new and aged buildings. Modernist urban planning assumed newer was always better, but older buildings maintain a sense of continuity on the streets.
- Finally, cities should foster a dense concentration of people. Urban planners held that large crowds were undesirable or

even dangerous. Jacobs, on the other hand, believed density and mixture make cities safer and more enjoyable.

Death and Life has sold more than 250,000 copies and undergone six translations.[3] Jacobs writes in a pithy, accessible style that reflected her populist stance—and though she was not an academic, *Death and Life* forever changed the discipline of urban studies* (an academic field focusing on the economics, planning, politics, transportation, and sociology* of urban environments).

Why Does *Death and Life* Matter?

Jacobs's criticism of urban planning exposed its many failures and reshaped how people understand cities; it also generated new insights into the process. Many cities answered her call to mix residential, commercial, industrial, and cultural spaces. Though Jacobs was not by any stretch a planner, *Death and Life* marked a turning point in urban studies and planning.

Real-world conflicts over urban space informed the analysis of *Death and Life*. Jacobs and other Greenwich Village residents attacked Robert Moses' vision, even though he ranked as the most influential urban planner of the times. In defeating Moses' proposal for a Lower Manhattan Expressway,* their movement made history—and shaped the analysis of *Death and Life*.[4] While Moses' plans usually revolved around automobiles and traffic, Jacobs reminded him and his colleagues that people should come first. Moses saw no value in street life; Jacobs argues that streets made cities great. Moses demolished old neighborhoods he saw as "slums"; Jacobs insists that these held more value and function than new suburbs. *Death and Life* stimulated academic debate while changing urban policy and politics in the process.

Jacobs offers several recommendations that many cities have since adopted.[5] She was among the first to suggest that mixed-use development,* with districts blending industrial, commercial, residential, and cultural space, improved city life. This countered the orthodoxy* (that is, the generally accepted practice) that cordoned off zones with different functions. Jacobs argues that a mix of aged and new buildings made for better streets. This defense of old buildings gave rise to an urban movement for historical preservation*—a movement to protect, preserve, and restore buildings, monuments, and objects with historic significance in urban areas. Even though urban planners saw large groups of people as a danger, Jacobs insists on the importance of these dense concentrations, arguing that this mix of people provided all cities with a source of vitality and creativity. Jacobs also maintains that this made cities safer. Mixture and density create "eyes on the street" that watch over neighborhoods.[6] Instead of urban chaos, Jacobs sees it as "organized complexity," giving a sense of order.[7] But urban planners, fearing congregation, separated and isolated people.

The ideas behind *Death and Life* have shaped urban policy, influenced historical preservation,[8] and highlighted the important economic functions that social interactions provide.[9] Where bureaucrats saw slums, decay, and expressways, Jacobs sees vitality, possibility, and a road to a different urban vision.

NOTES

1 Anthony Flint, *Wrestling with Moses: How Jane Jacobs Took on New York's Master Builder and Transformed the American City* (New York: Random House, 2009), 3–28.

2 Flint, *Wrestling with Moses*, 182.

3 Stephen Ward, "Obituary: Jane Jacobs." *The Independent*, June 3, 2006, accessed August 29, 2015, http://www.independent.co.uk/news/obituaries/jane-jacobs-6099183.html.

4 The links between *Death and Life* and Jacobs's activism in Greenwich Village are explored in Flint, *Wrestling with Moses*, 95–135.

5 For an assessment of Jacobs's legacy, see Roberta Brandes Gratz, *The Battle for Gotham: New York in the Shadow of Robert Moses and Jane Jacobs* (New York: Nation Books, 2010), 256–76.

6   Jane Jacobs, *The Death and Life of Great American Cities* (New York: Vintage Books, 1992), 35.

7   Jacobs, *Death and Life*, 429–39.

8   Gratz, *The Battle for Gotham*, 26–5.

9   Gratz, *The Battle for Gotham*, 266–8.

SECTION 1
INFLUENCES

MODULE 1
THE AUTHOR AND THE HISTORICAL CONTEXT

KEY POINTS

- *The Death and Life of Great American Cities* had an immediate impact with its searing condemnation of urban planning.* It continues to influence ideas and policies about city life.

- Jane Jacobs's observations of social interaction in Greenwich Village shaped her understanding of cities.

- While writing *Death and Life*, Jacobs joined Greenwich Village residents to save their neighborhoods from the architect and planner Robert Moses' reconstruction projects, which often proposed that neighborhoods be demolished to allow for the building of automobile infrastructure.

Why Read This Text?

Jane Jacobs's *The Death and Life of Great American Cities* (1961), with its blistering critique of architects such as Robert Moses—the "master builder" who transformed New York and its surrounding suburbs in the mid-twentieth century—challenged core ideas that dominated city planning and urban policy in the United States following World War II.* The work also instigated a paradigm shift (that is, a radical reappraisal) in urban planning after its 1961 publication. Jacobs developed an alternative view of city life, focusing on how people on the streets interact. Many cities have since implemented her proposals to mix residential, commercial, industrial, and cultural spaces.[1]

Death and Life presents a devastating assessment of urban planning in the period following World War II. It also anticipates many shifts in

> **❝** *The Death and Life of Great American Cities* hit the world of city planning like an earthquake when it was published in 1961. The book was a frontal attack on the planning establishment, especially on the massive urban renewal* projects that were being carried out by powerful redevelopment bureaucrats like Robert Moses* in New York. Jacobs derided urban renewal as a process that served only to create instant slums. **❞**
>
> Richard T. Le Gates and Frederic Stout, *The City Reader*

theory and policy that have occurred in the decades since the book's release. Jacobs's warnings about planning cities around automobile traffic have proven especially prophetic. By the time Jacobs wrote *Death and Life*, it had become clear that building more highways and expressways did not reduce traffic the way Moses and other planners promised. Jacobs saw that planning cities around cars and trucks devastated residential and downtown districts.[2] The erosion of communities and neighborhoods had become evident in the New York district of the South Bronx with the construction of the Cross Bronx Expressway.* Jacobs's criticism of Moses and other planners gave rise to an alternative urban transportation approach. Ideas like these from *Death and Life* have significantly influenced more contemporary forms of urban planning.[3]

Author's Life

Born in the city of Scranton in the US state of Pennsylvania in 1916, Jane Jacobs moved to New York City with her sister in 1934.[4] Although she was a professional journalist and writer, Jacobs never completed a degree or worked at a university.[5] She began writing about cities and architecture for *Architectural Forum** in the 1950s,[6] and when she wrote *Death and Life*, Jacobs lived in a renovated townhouse in the Lower Manhattan neighborhood of Greenwich Village.[7] *Death and Life* drew from her knowledge of cities, planning, and architecture, but also included what she observed from her home at 555 Hudson Street. In *Death and Life*, she wrote, "The stretch of Hudson Street where I live is each day the scene of an intricate sidewalk ballet."[8]

While writing *Death and Life*, Jacobs helped lead the movement to stop the construction of a Lower Manhattan Expressway.* The city's autocratic planner, Robert Moses, had conceived this highway, which would have bisected Washington Square Park,* a central place of recreation and cultural expression for village residents and those drawn to the neighborhood's bohemian character.[9] Jacobs chaired the Joint Committee to Stop the Lower Manhattan Expressway*—and was once arrested for destroying the stenographer's notes in protest at a public meeting in 1958.[10] A year after the publication of *Death and Life*, New York City officials were convinced by the movement to reject Moses' plan.[11]

Author's Background

After World War II, dominant ideas in urban planning involved slum clearance, the construction of high-rise public housing, and the creation of highways that linked cities with suburbs. This sort of urban planning separated residential, commercial, industrial, and cultural spaces. It razed whole neighborhoods for the sake of expressway traffic. And even though evidence of their failure mounted, these ideas had congealed into orthodoxy. The urban renewal movement developed over several decades from design and planning theories. Its roots took shape during the nineteenth century, a time when cities were seen as polluted, crowded, and generally undesirable places to live. Planners of that era introduced proposals and designs for utopian (that is, visionary and ideal) living and working spaces that sought to avoid the city's worst features.[12] They also presented urban renewal as a path to improve the economy and social life of cities, but Jacobs saw it as leading to the demise of everything that made cities work.

Contrary to the urban planners of her time, Jacobs argued that the life of cities stemmed from how people mixed on the streets. She contended that cities should include mixed-use spaces that combined industrial, commercial, residential, and cultural functions, while urban planners separated these into distinct districts. Her prescription for great cities also included short blocks that were easy to walk, a blend of old and new buildings, and a dense concentration of people. Where bureaucrats resorted to abstract theory, she relied on keen observation to inform her perspective: "People who are interested only in how a city 'ought' to look and uninterested in how it works will be disappointed by this book."[13] *Death and Life* mounted an unsparing attack on the ideas and policies that had held unquestioned acceptance among urban planners. It dashed their questionable projects and eventually eroded their false assumptions.

NOTES

1   A contemporary assessment of Jacobs's legacy can be found in Roberta Brandes Gratz, *The Battle for Gotham: New York in the Shadow of Robert Moses and Jane Jacobs* (New York: Nation Books, 2010), 256–76.

2   Anthony Flint, *Wrestling with Moses: How Jane Jacobs Took on New York's Master Builder and Transformed the American City* (New York: Random House, 2009), 62–3.

3   Gratz, *The Battle for Gotham*, 274–6.

4   Flint, *Wrestling with Moses*, 3–4.

5   Flint, *Wrestling with Moses*, 8–9.

6   Flint, *Wrestling with Moses*, 18.

7   Flint, *Wrestling with Moses*, 99.

8   Jane Jacobs, *The Death and Life of Great American Cities* (New York: Vintage Books, 1992), 50.

9   Flint, *Wrestling with Moses*, 62.

10 Flint, *Wrestling with Moses*, xiv.

11 Flint, *Wrestling with Moses*, 158–9.

12 Flint, *Wrestling with Moses*, 20.

13 Jacobs, *Death and Life*, 14.

MODULE 2
ACADEMIC CONTEXT

KEY POINTS

- Jane Jacobs challenged two schools of thought in urban planning: that of the Decentrists* (a group of urban theorists and planners from the nineteenth century who sought to reform the social and environmental ills of city life by decentralizing the population and built environment of cities); and that of the disciples of the influential Swiss French architect Le Corbusier.*

- Although it expressed concerns similar to hers, Jacobs did not engage with the Chicago School,* best known for its urban sociology (the study of the social constitution of urban environments). Associated with the sociology department at the University of Chicago, the Chicago School produced several groundbreaking studies of urban life in the 1920s and 1930s.

- While most of the observations in *The Death and Life of Great American Cities* came from New York City, Jacobs also noted that the same problems plagued other American cities.

The Work in its Context

In *The Death and Life of Great American Cities*, Jane Jacobs identified two schools of thought among urban planners. The first consisted of "Decentrists," and as the name implies, they sought to decentralize cities and disperse their people. Their main ideas came from the English urban theorist Ebenezer Howard* and the Scottish urban planner Sir Patrick Geddes,* who was noted for developing ideas that offered alternatives to the gridiron plans that dominated cities in his time. Conditions in London during the late nineteenth century

21

> **❝ I have been making unkind remarks about orthodox*** city planning theory, and shall make more as occasion arises to do so. By now, these orthodox ideas are part of our folklore. They harm us because we take them for granted. ❞
>
> Jane Jacobs, *The Death and Life of Great American Cities*

horrified Howard, who envisioned a "Garden City"* where people would create self-sufficient small towns in the countryside. Jacobs described how Howard's hostility towards cities shaped his urban planning: "He not only hated the wrongs and mistakes of the city, he hated the city and thought it was an outright evil and an affront that so many people should get themselves into an agglomeration. His prescription for saving the people was to do the city in."[1]

Writing in the early twentieth century, Geddes wanted to extend Howard's garden-city ideal into entire regions, distributing such municipalities outside urban areas.

The second school of thought derived from the famous Swiss French architect Le Corbusier, whose ideas reshaped Paris in the 1920s and 1930s. His ideal Radiant City* called for a succession of skyscrapers standing in a park. As Jacobs wrote, "His city was like a wonderful mechanical toy ... It was so orderly, so visible, so easy to understand. It said everything in a flash, like a good advertisement."[2] While the Decentrists influenced planning outside the city, Le Corbusier's ideas informed what went on inside it. His influence appears most evident in high-rise office buildings and low-income housing projects.

Overview of the Field

Jacobs criticized both the Decentrists and the disciples of Le

Corbusier. Howard's garden city assumed that a dense concentration of people was an inherent evil, whereas for Jacobs, dense concentration provided a source of vitality and creativity. Jacobs also dismissed Howard's vision of planned communities as "paternalistic, if not authoritarian."[3] While the Decentrists and the Le Corbusier school held different visions of the ideal community, both reflected a top-down approach. Le Corbusier's notion of Utopia was more libertarian; as Jacobs described it, "In his Radiant City nobody, presumably, was going to have to be his brother's keeper any more."[4] The Decentrists shaped the growth of the suburbs, while Le Corbusier's vision was most evident in New York City and Moses' planning.

As Jacobs could have used academic backup for her ideas, it is curious that she never addressed the Chicago School, known for its urban sociology. The scholars of the Chicago School, amongst whom were the founding urban sociologists Robert Park,* Louis Wirth,* and Ernest Burgess,* conducted their research at the University of Chicago during the 1920s and 1930s and are notable for their influence on the field of urban studies.*

Jacobs's lack of engagement with Park and Wirth is surprising, as social interaction within cities interested both men. Like Jacobs, Park had a background in journalism (though in Chicago) and encouraged his students to research urban life using an ethnographic (study of people and cultures) approach. Jacobs might have gleaned more insights if she had considered the work of the Chicago School, particularly Park's and Wirth's observations.

Academic Influences

Jane Jacobs was not an academic, and prevailing urban planning theories influenced her only in a negative sense. Bureaucratic failures compelled Jacobs to investigate what truly worked in cities. She credited a social worker with initiating the questions behind *Death and Life*: "The basic idea, to try to begin understanding the intricate social and economic order under the seeming disorder of the cities, was not my idea at all, but that of William Kirk, head worker of Union Settlement in East Harlem, New York, who, by showing me East Harlem, showed me a way of seeing other neighborhoods, and downtowns too."[5]

Jacobs also noted that Kirk called her attention to "the intricate social and economic order beneath the seeming disorder of cities."[6] Jacobs learned more about cities through observation than by studying theory. She rejected the authoritarian—dictatorial—nature of planners, insisting that communities and their residents knew best.

Because Jacobs based her analysis on observation, it makes sense that so many of her examples come from New York City and her Greenwich Village neighborhood. Yet other American cities followed New York's lead in urban renewal, with the same negative results. (Chicago's Eisenhower Expressway, for example, destroyed entire neighborhoods as it carved the nearby western suburb of Oak Park cleanly in half.) Jacobs explained that she first saw many of these trends in other cities: "In trying to explain the underlying order of cities, I use a preponderance of examples from New York because that is where I live. But most of the basic ideas in this book come from things I first noticed or was told in other cities."[7] Jacobs realized that New York City had become a "model" for other cities across the United States, where the growing list of failures derived from the same flawed assumptions. What the planners broke and could not then fix, she sought to set straight.

NOTES

1   Jane Jacobs, *The Death and Life of Great American Cities* (New York: Vintage Books, 1992), 17.

2   Jacobs, *Death and Life*, 23.

3   Jacobs, *Death and Life*, 19.

4   Jacobs, *Death and Life*, 22.

5   Jacobs, *Death and Life*, 15–16.

6   Jacobs, *Death and Life*, 15.

7   Jacobs, *Death and Life*, 15.

MODULE 3
THE PROBLEM

KEY POINTS

- Jane Jacobs's main question was whether urban renewal helped or harmed cities. If it caused harm, she wanted to know which alternatives cities should pursue.

- When Jacobs wrote *The Death and Life of Great American Cities*, planners took the benefits of urban renewal for granted.

- Jacobs rejected the ideas of urban planning.* She insisted that observing social interaction was crucial for understanding cities.

Core Question

Jane Jacobs sought to answer one core question in *The Death and Life of Great American Cities*: was urban renewal good for cities—and if not, then what should cities do instead? To find answers, she had to tackle the larger issue of what makes cities work in the first place. Urban planners took these questions and their answers for granted. The biggest critics of planning were people living in the communities that urban renewal had devastated. Jacobs sided with their perspective, arguing, "Planners frequently seem to be less well equipped intellectually for respecting and understanding particulars than ordinary people, untrained in expertise, who are attached to a neighborhood, accustomed to using it, and so are not accustomed to thinking of it in generalized or abstract fashion."[1]

Jacobs had faith in a community's ability to understand cities better than planners—who never questioned the central tenets of urban planning the way Jacobs did. She asked critical questions about urban

> 66 Jacobs derided urban renewal* as a process that served only to create instant slums. She questioned universally accepted articles of faith—for example that parks were good and that crowding was bad. Instead she suggested that parks were often dangerous and that crowded neighborhood sidewalks were the safest places for children to play. 99
>
> Richard T. LeGates and Frederic Stout, *The City Reader*

renewal that stemmed from neighborhood movements. Local protests in the 1950s fought the construction of the Cross Bronx Expressway,* a significant automobile route across the borough of New York known as the Bronx designed by the architect and planner Robert Moses.* After Jacobs read about Moses' plans to extend Fifth Avenue through the middle of Washington Square Park, she joined the Washington Square Park Committee,* founded by the community organizer Shirley Hayes.*[2] *Death and Life* found a wide audience because Jacobs gave voice to the growing sense of discontent about urban renewal— and instigated controversy because she challenged its basic assumptions.

The Participants

Jacobs attacked both the "city-destroying ideas" of the Decentrists and the urban planning of Le Corbusier.[3]

The Decentrists' ideas originated with Ebenezer Howard's model of the garden city,* and they favored a planning approach that stemmed from a dislike of cities and their dense concentrations of people. In Jacobs's time, the most influential disciple of the Decentrists was Lewis Mumford,* an architecture critic for *The New Yorker** magazine. Mumford had written a book titled *The Culture of Cities*, which Jacobs derided as "a morbid and biased catalog of ills."[4] He responded with a review of *Death and Life* titled "Mother Jacobs Home Remedies."[5] Mumford's review acknowledged the significance of *Death and Life* and the novelty of its criticism, yet it had a condescending and even chauvinistic tone, as he labeled her approach "naked unawareness" and described it as "a mingling of sense and sentimentality, of mature judgments and schoolgirl howlers."[6]

Robert Moses never issued a public comment about *Death and Life*, though he returned the copy sent to him by its publisher, Random House, accompanied by a stern letter to the company's co-founder. "I am returning the book you sent me," Moses wrote. "Aside from the fact that it is intemperate and inaccurate, it is also libelous … Sell this junk to someone else."[7] *Death and Life* clearly touched a nerve in the man who considered himself New York's master builder.

The Contemporary Debate

When Jacobs wrote *Death and Life*, planners by and large did not question the wisdom of urban renewal—but her thinking about what makes cities great challenged their assumptions. Saskia Sassen,* a professor at Columbia University, argues that theorists had once seen the city as a "lens for understanding larger processes, a role it had lost by the 1950s."[8] However, in time, Jacobs's ideas gained greater acceptance as some planners began to incorporate her suggestions. In sum, "Jacobs's ideas have had a strong impact on the way urbanists and planners think about city life."[9] Following the publication of *Death and Life*, urban renewal came under greater scrutiny as planners and architects began to pay more attention to the dynamics of social interaction in cities.[10] In this way, Jacobs was truly ahead of her time.

Likewise, scholars who research cities and develop theories about them adopted more of Jacobs's ideas. *Death and Life* later became a foundational text for the school of thought known as New Urbanism,*[11] and scholars began to reconsider Jacobs's work in the light of gentrification,* the process whereby wealthy professionals migrate to central urban neighborhoods. Her ideas about mixed-use development,* aged buildings, and vibrant street life influenced the gentrification process—and as gentrification displaced working-class families, Jacobs's inattention to power and inequality came under scrutiny;[12] similarly, she failed to consider the ways in which race, ethnicity, class, and gender also shape how people experience the city. Yet her adversaries in the planning world never even bothered to consider people in the first place, and since then, these key questions of power and inequality have become central to urban studies.

NOTES

1 Jane Jacobs, *The Death and Life of Great American Cities* (New York: Vintage Books, 1992), 441.

2 Anthony Flint, *Wrestling with Moses: How Jane Jacobs Took on New York's Master Builder and Transformed the American City* (New York: Random House, 2009), 75.

3 Jacobs, *Death and Life*, 17.

4 Jacobs, *Death and Life*, 20.

5 Lewis Mumford, "The Sky Line: 'Mother Jacobs Home Remedies,'" *The New Yorker*, December 1, 1962.

6 Kenneth Kidd, "Did Jane Jacobs' Critics Have a Point After All?" *The Toronto Star*, November 25, 2011, accessed August 31, 2015, http://www.thestar.com/news/insight/2011/11/25/did_jane_jacobs_critics_have_a_point_after_all.html.

7 Flint, *Wrestling with Moses*, 125.

8 Saskia Sassen, "What Would Jane Jacobs See in the Global City? Place and Social Practices," in *The Urban Wisdom of Jane Jacobs*, ed. Sonia Hirt and Diana Zahm (New York: Routledge, 2012), 84.

9 Mark Gottdiener, Ray Hutchinson, and Michael T. Ryan, *The New Urban Sociology*, 5th edn (Boulder, CO: Westview Press), 328.

10 Roberta Brandes Gratz, *The Battle for Gotham: New York in the Shadow of Robert Moses and Jane Jacobs* (New York: Nation Books, 2010).

11 Peter Katz, *The New Urbanism: Toward an Architecture of Community* (New York: McGraw-Hill Education, 1993).

12 Sharon Zukin, "Changing Landscapes of Power: Opulence and the Urge for Authenticity," *International Journal of Urban and Regional Research* 33, no. 2 (2009): 548–9.

MODULE 4
THE AUTHOR'S CONTRIBUTION

KEY POINTS

- Jane Jacobs aimed to show how cities work by investigating questions urban planners* had ignored.
- Urban planners assumed that cities were problematic and needed renewal. Sociologists from the Chicago School, an approach associated with the sociology* department at the University of Chicago, also maintained that cities were undesirable.
- Jacobs examined what made cities work because she could see that urban planning destroyed rather than renewed them.

Author's Aims

In *The Death and Life of American Cities*, Jane Jacobs seeks to understand and explain what makes cities great for the people who live in them. The work posed questions urban planners had failed to ask, largely because they assumed cities were undesirable places to live. Postwar policies supported a migration of the population into new suburbs, while planners promoted forms of urban renewal that devastated city neighborhoods.

Planners took an abstract view of cities that all but ignored the lives and needs of their inhabitants. Instead, they concerned themselves with the height of buildings, the creation of green spaces, and the efficient flow of traffic. Jacobs redefines their questions by returning the focus to how people used urban spaces. "I shall mainly be writing about common ordinary things," she writes at the beginning of *Death and Life*.[1] She then lists her concerns, which include:

- the safety of city streets

❝ Jane Jacobs's ideas have influenced urbanists because she captured the heart and soul of urban culture. Her importance lies in convincing us that urban culture depends on the relationship between personal interaction and public space. **❞**

Mark Gottdiener, Ray Hutchison, and Michael T. Ryan, *The New Urban Sociology*

- the quality of city parks
- the condition of slums, and why they sometimes regenerated despite powerful opposition
- the shifting concerns of downtown districts
- the character and function of city neighborhoods.[2]

Jacobs succeeded in shifting the terms of the debate about cities. She based her findings on observation and as a result reached vastly different conclusions to those of the urban planners.

Approach

Jacobs broke new ground because she focused on how people interacted with and used city spaces. Her approach stood as the complete antithesis of urban planning's abstract theorizing. Urban planners saw little of value in city life, condemned entire neighborhoods as "slums," and set about destroying them. For them, the good life existed far from urban America, in small towns and suburbs. But Jacobs revealed how cities crackled with vitality, innovation, and diversity. "For Jacobs," in brief, "active urban life can never be planned because people invent uses for space."[3]

The inventiveness of *Death and Life* stemmed from Jacobs's methods for studying urban life. She watched how her neighbors went about their daily routines and observed that a city's social order "is kept primarily by an intricate, almost unconscious, network of voluntary controls and standards among the people themselves, and enforced by the people themselves."[4] In other words, social interaction on city streets creates a form of order that planners and architects cannot design.

In contrast, she saw how high-rise housing projects had become anonymous and dangerous. About such places she wrote, "No amount of police can enforce civilization where the normal, casual enforcement of it has broken down."[5] She also noted how the postwar suburbs produced monotony and demanded conformity—a view ahead of its time that wouldn't be embraced for decades. By focusing on the human scale of city life—and using original observational methods—Jacobs reached novel conclusions that flew in the face of urban planning's impersonal model.

Contribution in Context

Few scholars had studied urban life through routine social interaction, and so the originality of *Death and Life* came from Jacobs's street-level analysis, which flipped the top-down approach of urban planners on its head. While Jacobs did not engage with the Chicago School, known for urban sociology, its members had asked similar questions. The Chicago School focused more on urban subcultures than on the built environment of the city, with the sociologist Louis Wirth* of the University of Chicago more concerned with *urbanism* as a way of life than with *urbanization* as a physical transformation. For Wirth, urbanism's three characteristics were aggregate population size, density, and heterogeneity (which refers to its internal differences in things such as character, use, and population).[6]

Death and Life proved original because Jacobs not only studied cities at the street level but drew positive conclusions. Both planners and ethnographers—those studying a place's inhabitants—had assumed urban life was undesirable. Even urban sociologists of the

Chicago School tended to view urbanism as a social ill, while planners in the years following World War II* advocated the depopulation of cities in favor of suburban living. Jacobs's aim, remarkable for its time, was to show how cities could foster both creativity and community. Figures such as Robert Moses* looked at city neighborhoods as chaotic slums begging for demolition and renewal. Jacobs argued that although city people were poor, these neighborhoods served as dynamic centers of interaction. Instead of renewing them, urban planning did quite the opposite, leaving countless corners of America's cities more anonymous, desolate, and alienating.

NOTES

1   Jane Jacobs, *The Death and Life of Great American Cities* (New York: Vintage Books, 1992), 3–4.

2   Jacobs, *Death and Life*, 3–4.

3   Mark Gottdiener, Ray Hutchison, and Michael T. Ryan, *The New Urban Sociology*, 5th edn (Boulder, CO: Westview Press, 2015), 327.

4   Jacobs, *Death and Life*, 32.

5   Jacobs, *Death and Life*, 32.

6   Louis Wirth, "Urbanism as a Way of Life," *American Journal of Sociology*, 44, no. 1 (July 1938): 1–24.

SECTION 2
IDEAS

MODULE 5
MAIN IDEAS

KEY POINTS

- Jane Jacobs's main argument is that urban planners ruin cities because they fail to consider the city's dynamics of social interaction—the ways in which a city is defined by different social interactions in different contexts.

- Jacobs opposed the segregating, standardizing approach of urban planning.* She insisted that diversity, concentration, and mixture make cities great.

- Jacobs wrote *The Death and Life of Great American Cities* in direct, plain-spoken prose. This reflected her populist criticism of abstract urban theory.

Key Themes

The Death and Life of Great American Cities argues that urban planning destroys the vitality of city life. Jane Jacobs maintains that planners failed because they did not understand how social interaction creates great cities. While they presented urban renewal* to the public as a form of progress, Jacobs argued that it actually left cities worse off and more dangerous than before. Writing in 1961, she assesses what had become of cities in the wake of urban renewal: "Low-income projects that become worse centers of delinquency, vandalism, and general social hopelessness than the slums they were supposed to replace ... Promenades that go from no place to nowhere and have no promenaders. Expressways that eviscerate great cities. This is not the rebuilding of cities. This is the sacking of cities."[1]

❝ This book is an attack on current city planning and rebuilding. It is also, and mostly, an attempt to introduce new principles of city planning and rebuilding, different and even opposite from those now taught in everything from schools to architecture and planning to the Sunday supplements and women's magazines. ❞

Jane Jacobs, *The Death and Life of Great American Cities*

Jacobs develops four key themes in *Death and Life*:
- Urban renewal does not renew cities but actually destroys them.
- Planners ignore the everyday realities of social life in the city.
- Interaction of people on the streets makes cities "great."
- Great cities are built on diversity, concentration, and mixture instead of separation and standardization.

Because planners devised proposals and policies mainly from urban theory, they neglected to consider the micro-social dynamics of life in the city—the interactions between individuals. Jacobs saw this as a kind of futuristic fantasy that promised a more modern way of life but predictably resulted in failure and misery: "The pseudoscience of city planning and its companion, the art of city design, have not yet broken with the specious comforts of wishes, familiar superstitions, oversimplifications, and symbols, and have not yet embarked upon the adventure of probing the real world."[2]

Instead of using powers of observation, bureaucrats (office-bound city officials) fixated on buildings and expressways, without ever taking into account the people affected by their construction.

Exploring the Ideas

Jacobs's damning criticisms reflected a different perspective gleaned through what she witnessed in her own neighborhood of New York's Greenwich Village. She insists that the life of any city lies in the commonplace actions and interactions of its millions of people—in which case urban planning can only succeed when its proposals take these social dynamics into account. Jacobs writes, "Cities have the capability of providing something for everybody, only because, and only when, they are created by everybody."[3] It is, she argues, entire communities of people engaging in interaction that creates great cities, and not a team of expert architects.

Yet these professionals and public officials lobbied for separation and standardization, which split commercial, residential, industrial, and cultural spaces. This led to homogeneous, sterile suburbs outside the city limits and anonymous, isolated housing projects within them. In contrast, Jacobs insists that diversity, concentration, and mixture made cities great. "To understand cities," Jacobs argues, "we have to deal outright with combinations or mixtures of uses, not separate uses, as the essential phenomena."[4] Against the prevailing wisdom, Jacobs contends that cities should incorporate spaces with mixed uses. This idea has been quite influential in contemporary urban planning,[5] while the conventions she fought against are today dismissed as incompatible with the creation of vibrant cities.

Diversity, concentration, and mixture also apply to people in the city and how they interact ("People gathered in concentrations of city size and density can be considered a positive good,"[6] Jacobs writes). Density maintains a strong connection to diversity, another facet of urban life that Jacobs valued but that planners of her era tended to dread. Jacobs maintains that the interaction between distinct kinds of people played an important role in creating vitality in cities, as she champions "a great and exuberant richness of differences and possibilities, many of these differences unique and unpredictable and all the more valuable because they are."[7]

Language and Expression

Jane Jacobs had little patience for the so-called experts who designed cities in abstraction from real life. She believed cities represented collections of ordinary people and commonplace actions. Likewise, she wrote *Death and Life* in plain, simple prose that avoids the jargon and cold language of urban planning and theory. Jacobs's concise, direct, and straightforward style jumps out right from the first sentence of *Death and Life*: "This book is an attack on current city planning and rebuilding."[8] The plain-spoken form of Jacobs's writing was a perfect match for the populist content of her critique.

Jacobs came to the study of cities and urban planning not as an academic, but as a journalist and New York City resident. This, along with the commonplace nature of her observations, gave *Death and Life* a degree of accessibility akin to that of a well-written magazine article. Jacobs began working as a journalist in the early 1940s, later writing for the journal *Architectural Forum*.* As Anthony Flint would write in his book *Wrestling With Moses*, "Jacobs was a natural for all aspects of journalism and magazine publishing—a stickler for details, an authority on proper writing style and grammar, highly organized, and good at coming up with story ideas."[9] Jacobs brought her extraordinary talents as a journalist and a writer to bear in *Death and Life*, resulting in a devastating critique that brought down a planned expressway, and gave rise to a visionary view of cities.

NOTES

1   Jane Jacobs, *The Death and Life of Great American Cities* (New York: Vintage Books, 1992), 4.

2   Jacobs, *Death and Life*, 13.

3   Jacobs, *Death and Life*, 238.

4   Jacobs, *Death and Life*, 144.

5   Roberta Brandes Gratz, *The Battle for Gotham: New York in the Shadow of Robert Moses and Jane Jacobs* (New York: Nation Books, 2010), 256–76.

6   Jacobs, *Death and Life*, 220–1.

7   Jacobs, *Death and Life*, 220–1.

8   Jacobs, *Death and Life*, 3.

9   Anthony Flint, *Wrestling with Moses: How Jane Jacobs Took on New York's Master Builder and Transformed the American City* (New York: Random House, 2009), 10.

MODULE 6
SECONDARY IDEAS

KEY POINTS

- Jane Jacobs offers several recommendations to supplement her critique of urban planning.* These consist of mixed-use development* (spaces where industrial, commercial, and cultural activities occur), short blocks, aged buildings, and dense concentration.
- As they embraced her critique, contemporary urban planners have adopted many of Jacobs's suggestions.
- Jacobs's advocacy of mixed-use spaces has had the largest impact on contemporary urban planning.

Other Ideas

Jane Jacobs's *The Death and Life of Great American Cities* primarily concerns itself with the effects of urban renewal.* In explaining why urban renewal failed, Jacobs investigates the opposite side of the coin: what makes cities work and what had once made them great. Where urban planners saw diversity as a source of chaos and disorder, Jacobs countered that it was a source of strength and vitality.

While *Death and Life* delivers a blistering critique of urban renewal, it offers smart alternatives; in the work's second part, Jacobs outlines four conditions that create diversity in cities:

- First, districts should include more than one primary function, thereby creating mixed-use spaces.
- Second, most blocks should be short, allowing more opportunities to turn corners.
- Third, districts are best when buildings vary in age and condition.

> **❝** Under the seeming disorder of the old city, wherever the old city is working successfully, is a marvelous order for maintaining the safety of the streets and the freedom of the city. It is a complex order. Its essence is intricacy of sidewalk use, bringing with it a succession of eyes. **❞**
>
> Jane Jacobs, *The Death and Life of Great American Cities*

- Fourth, there should be a sufficiently dense concentration of people.

Jacobs argues that all four conditions must be present to foster diversity, and so the absence of any one of them would limit the others. "The potentials of different districts differ for many reasons," she acknowledges, "but, given the development of these four conditions, a city district should be able to realize its best potential, wherever that may lie."[1] Not all cities are the same, but Jacobs believes that any of them could benefit from these four suggestions.

Exploring the Ideas

Urban planners preferred to separate residential, commercial, industrial, and cultural zones. However, mixed-use development, Jacobs contends, would ensure the circulation of people at various times of the day. Spaces with multiple uses attract "the presence of people who go outdoors on different schedules and are in the place for different purposes, but who are able to use many facilities in common."[2] When people occupy the streets at all times of the day, neighborhoods become safer and local businesses prosper.

Short blocks have a similar importance for stimulating diversity. The long streets and discrete neighborhoods urban planners created led to isolated, stagnant, and dangerous stretches. In contrast, Jacobs argues, "frequent streets and short blocks are valuable because of the fabric of intricate cross-use that they permit among the users of a city neighborhood." Short blocks enable the movement and mixture of pedestrians who use the same streets for different purposes.[3]

Jacobs's claim that cities need aged buildings went against both the grain of urban planning and the ideals of postwar modernism—which celebrated the new while disparaging the old in many forms of art and culture. Bureaucrats and their architects looked at neighborhoods with old buildings as blighted. However, while they promoted the process of demolition and renewal as progress, Jacobs counters, "If a city has only new buildings, the enterprises that can exist there are automatically limited to those that can support the high costs of construction."[4] She argues that preserving old buildings is essential to protect local businesses that can survive in them—and that would be crippled by the high overhead of new construction.

Jacobs's fourth condition of diversity involves dense concentrations of people. Once again, she goes against the prevailing ideas of the urban-planning establishment—after all, planners despised and feared population density. But Jacobs believes that density is one of the most important factors in making cities interesting and vital places—and insists that an abundance of people gives the city its unique character: "They should also be enjoyed as an asset and their presence celebrated: by raising their concentrations where it is needful for flourishing city life, and beyond that by aiming for a visibly lively public street life and for accommodating and encouraging, economically and visually, as much variety as possible."[5]

Overlooked

Many planners have since adopted Jacobs's recipe for fostering diversity. Her ideas, which once attracted the scorn of the planning establishment, have actually become part of mainstream planning. As a result, their original links with community organizing (as opposed to elite expertise) are now forgotten. Jacobs argues that communities know best, but this insight dissipated once planners started to utilize her ideas. In short, "Often overlooked is Jacobs' influence on community organizing … Jacobs' activist work showed people around the country that they could fight against the urban renewal bulldozer—and win."[6] Contemporary urbanists have credited Jacobs for changing the debate about how to plan cities. Yet they have neglected to recognize how her ideas emerged within a larger community engaged in a political struggle.

Another overlooked aspect of *Death and Life* concerns the relationship between women and the city. Writing in 1961, Jacobs's analysis predated by several years the emergence of second-wave feminism* (the social movement of women that began in the late 1960s, continuing earlier struggles for nondiscrimination, reproductive rights, and social equality). As the political scientist Marshall Berman* argued, "She makes her readers feel that women know what it is like to live in cities, street by street, day by day, far better than the men who plan and build them."[7] By focusing on the commonplace activities that occur on a daily basis, Jacobs shows herself as more attuned to a woman's perspective of city life. For Berman, she "gives us the first fully articulated woman's view of the city since [the social reformer] Jane Addams.*"[8]

Mainstream geographers and planners often bypass the feminism of Jacobs's critique because it preceded the second wave of feminism. Nevertheless, *Death and Life* features a feminist perspective on a crucial social and political topic that bears witness to how much a determined, visionary woman can achieve in the face of an entrenched male hierarchy.

NOTES

1   Jane Jacobs, *The Death and Life of Great American Cities* (New York: Vintage Books, 1992), 151.

2   Jacobs, *Death and Life*, 152.

3   Jacobs, *Death and Life*, 186.

4   Jacobs, *Death and Life*, 187.

5   Jacobs, *Death and Life*, 221.

6   Peter Dreier, "Jane Jacobs' Radical Legacy," *National Housing Institute* 146 (Summer 2006), accessed September 5, 2015, http://www.nhi.org/online/issues/146/janejacobslegacy.html.

7   Marshall Berman, *All That Is Solid Melts into Air: The Experience of Modernity* (New York: Penguin Books, 1982), 322.

8   Berman, *All That Is Solid Melts into Air*, 322.

MODULE 7
ACHIEVEMENT

KEY POINTS

- Jane Jacobs exposed and shattered the fundamental premises of the reconstructive policies of urban renewal* following World War II.*

- Jacobs's argument prevailed because she articulated popular dissatisfaction with urban renewal.

- Because she failed to consider economic factors alongside political ones, Jacobs left no basis for a critique of gentrification*—the process whereby wealthy professionals migrate to regenerating urban neighborhoods, pricing out the existing residents.

Assessing the Argument

Jane Jacobs's *The Death and Life of Great American Cities* is now regarded as a classic in urban studies,* and is often cited as a key text in the fields of urban sociology,* geography, and architecture.

Her recommendations are also frequently implemented in policy, as noted in a recent book, *The New Urban Sociology*: "Jacobs's ideas have had a strong impact on the way urbanists and planners think about city life. Local governments encourage park use, street festivals, temporary blocking of community roads, and toleration of sidewalk vendors."[1] Indeed, few books have made so many contributions to theory and practice in such a number of disciplines. The publication of *Death and Life* marked a turning point for urban studies.

Still, not all the ideas in *Death and Life* have proven acceptable or successful. nAs the coauthors of *The New Urban Sociology* note, "Some of her followers advocated the elimination of elevators in apartment

> ❝ The great urban theorist Jane Jacobs was not an academically trained economist, but her theory of growth made an indelible contribution to the field. In her eyes, it was new types of work and new ways of doing things that drove large-scale economic expansions. But while most economists located momentum in great companies, entrepreneurs, and nation-states, Jacobs identified great cities as the prime motor force behind innovation. ❞
>
> Richard Florida, *The Rise of the Creative Class*

buildings to facilitate neighborly interaction, but the results were disastrous for the residents of these buildings."[2] One crucial deterrent to the implementation of Jacobs's ideas is crime. So it was that, in many cities, "downtown revitalization efforts using Jacobs's ideas have failed due to the fear of urban crime on the part of suburban residents."[3] Finally, permeating *Death and Life* is a strong streak of sentimentality and nostalgia that no longer pertains to city life. In sum, "Jacobs's ideas about community may also be passé. Many city residents socialize with networks of friends and relatives who do not live nearby ... Teenagers may prefer to travel to their own friendship networks rather than socialize on the street."[4]

Achievement in Context

Jacobs wrote *Death and Life* at a time when communities began to challenge urban renewal. These social circumstances bolstered the book's success. Neighborhood movements arose in the New York borough of the Bronx during the 1950s in opposition to the building of a major road, the Cross Bronx Expressway,* and *Death and Life* appeared in 1961 as residents fought the architect and planner Robert Moses'* plans for urban renewal in Lower Manhattan. *Death and Life* articulated a new way of thinking about cities: "It became an inspiration, guidebook, and bible for not only a new generation of planners and architects but ordinary citizens as well."[5] These external events of political conflict made *Death and Life* one of the most urgent books of its time.

Death and Life was the first of several books to impact social issues and public policy in the early 1960s. Other books published shortly afterwards that roused public awareness included the marine biologist and environmentalist Rachel Carson's* *Silent Spring* (1962); the social campaigner Michael Harrington's* *The Other America* (1962); the feminist author Betty Friedan's* *The Feminine Mystique* (1963); and the activist and consumer advocate Ralph Nader's* *Unsafe at Any Speed* (1965). Carson's *Silent Spring* helped launch environmentalism with its exposé of pesticide use.[6] Harrington's *The Other America* provided a catalyst for the War on Poverty.[7] *The Feminine Mystique* became a foundational text for second-wave feminism; Friedan would establish the National Organization for Women (NOW)* in 1966.[8] And Nader's *Unsafe at Any Speed* exposed the auto industry's evasion of safety precautions (using the American car manufacturer Chevrolet's Corvair as a focal point) and provided the impetus for consumer advocacy.[9]

Death and Life also offered a rationale for the "back to the city" movement that anticipated gentrification. Starting in the 1950s, middle-class professionals in New York began relocating to formerly working-class neighborhoods in the borough of Brooklyn such as Brooklyn Heights, Park Slope, and Boerum Hill, where they renovated period houses.[10] Jacobs's book became an influential text for them following its publication: "Most of the middle-class enthusiasts inspired to move to Brooklyn by Jane Jacobs' *Death and Life of Great American Cities* cited her sentimental 'street ballet' or the passages where she slipped into simple romantic nostalgia."[11] An unanticipated effect of *Death and Life* was its stimulation of gentrification—which contemporary critics have blamed for displacing the working class and the poor, people of color, and ethnic communities from urban neighborhoods.

Limitations

In the decades following the publication of *Death and Life*, scholars have identified at least two major shortcomings. First, Jacobs does not pay attention to the economic factors that drive urban development. Although she distrusted the state power embodied by Robert Moses, capitalist developers escaped her critique. And so, while "Jacobs and other [residents of the neighborhood of Greenwich Village] were busy fighting off Moses' large-scale public works plans, they failed to oppose the quieter, piecemeal incursions of private real estate developers, who through the 1950s were demolishing older buildings all over the Village for new high-rises."[12] Though *Death and Life* presented a devastating assessment of urban renewal, Jacobs's inattention to capitalist development ensured her complicity with gentrification.

A second limitation concerns Jacobs's nostalgic ideal of great cities, in which older neighborhoods are seen as being more close-knit and down to earth than their suburban successors. This derives from the authenticity of ethnic neighborhoods that Jacobs imagines. In the years after *Death and Life*, gentrifying professionals returned to the city in search of this authenticity. In brief, "Jacobs fails to recognize the growing influence of her own perspective, to see that families like hers are gradually moving to the West Village's nineteenth century houses because they appreciate the charm of the area's little shops and cobblestone streets."[13] In other words, Jacobs idealized older cities and urban communities in ways later emulated by young, white-collar professionals who gentrified American cities such as Chicago and San Francisco. The irony of gentrification is that it uproots the ethnic and artistic enclaves that professionals picture as the embodiment of authenticity.

NOTES

1   Mark Gottdiener, Ray Hutchison, and Michael T. Ryan, *The New Urban Sociology*, 5th edn (Boulder, CO: Westview Press, 2015), 328.

2   Gottdiener, Hutchison, and Ryan, *The New Urban Sociology*, 328.

3   Gottdiener, Hutchison, and Ryan, *The New Urban Sociology*, 328.

4   Gottdiener, Hutchison, and Ryan, *The New Urban Sociology*, 328.

5   Anthony Flint, *Wrestling with Moses: How Jane Jacobs Took on New York's Master Builder and Transformed the American City* (New York: Random House, 2009), 129.

6   Rachel Carson, *Silent Spring* (Boston: Houghton Mifflin Company, 1962).

7   Michael Harrington, *The Other America: Poverty in the United States* (New York: Touchstone, 1962).

8   Betty Friedan, *The Feminine Mystique* (New York: W. W. Norton, 1963).

9   Ralph Nader, *Unsafe at Any Speed: The Designed-In Dangers of the American Automobile* (New York: Grossman, 1965).

10 Suleiman Osman, *The Invention of Brownstone Brooklyn: Gentrification and the Search for Authenticity in Postwar New York* (New York: Oxford University Press, 2011).

11 Osman, *The Invention of Brownstone Brooklyn*, 169.

12 John Strausbaugh, *The Village: A History of Greenwich Village* (New York: HarperCollins, 2013), 341.

13 Sharon Zukin, *Naked City: The Death and Life of Authentic Urban Places* (New York: Oxford University Press, 2010), 18.

MODULE 8
PLACE IN THE AUTHOR'S WORK

KEY POINTS

- Jane Jacobs had a wide range of interests, but throughout her life she focused on cities and their economies.
- Although she wrote six more books, *The Death and Life of Great of American Cities* remained her most well known.
- *Death and Life* established Jacobs's international reputation as an authority on cities and urban living.

Positioning

The Death and Life of Great American Cities certainly qualifies as Jane Jacobs's best-known work. She had outlined some of the book's major themes in an earlier article, "Downtown Is for People," published by *Fortune* magazine in 1958. Jacobs had given a talk for the Conference on Urban Design at Harvard University's Graduate School of Design, and *Fortune* writer and editor William H. Whyte* asked her to develop it into an article. In "Downtown Is for People," Jacobs presented her main critique of urban renewal: "These projects will not revitalize downtown; they will deaden it ... They will be stable and symmetrical and orderly. They will be clean, impressive, and monumental. They will have all the attributes of a well-kept, dignified cemetery."[1] The *Fortune* article stated some of her arguments against urban renewal,* but she had yet to define what made cities work.

Death and Life was Jacobs's first of seven books, most of which focused on cities and urban development. She began writing her second book, *The Economy of Cities*, during her years of activism in New York, and completed it shortly after moving to Toronto. In a chapter titled "The Valuable Inefficiencies and Impracticalities of

❝ None of [her other] books were blockbusters like *The Death and Life of Great American Cities*, and Jacobs began to chafe when the questions inexorably led back to her days among the bohemians in Greenwich Village, fighting the New York battles—as if she were a rock star constantly being asked to play an old hit. **❞**

Anthony Flint, *Wrestling with Moses: How Jane Jacobs Took on New York's Master Builder and Transformed the American City*

Cities," Jacobs compared the economies of the English cities Manchester and Birmingham. While Manchester teetered on the brink of becoming an "obsolescent city," Birmingham's "fragmented and inefficient little industries kept adding new work, and splitting off new organizations, some of which became very large but were still outweighed in total employment and production by the many small ones." *The Economy of Cities* continued to develop a central conclusion she had reached in *Death and Life*: diversity was crucial to the life of cities, while large-scale projects were counterproductive.[2]

Integration

The rest of Jacobs's books explored a range of other concerns, often departing from the analysis of cities and their economies. Her third book, 1980's *The Question of Separatism*, made a case for the French-speaking region of Quebec's independence from Canada.[3] Although this book digressed from her concern with cities, it continued the advocacy of popular self-determination that began with *Death and Life*. Her next book, *Cities and the Wealth of Nations*, revisited the topic of urban economics, but her fifth, *Systems of Survival*, explored new questions of morality and values.[4] *Systems of Survival* examined the different moral precepts behind what Jacobs labeled a "guardian syndrome" and a "commerce syndrome." She returned to the study of economics in *The Nature of Economies*, but her final book, *Dark Age Ahead*, was an apocalyptic warning about the decay of North American society.[5]

Although Jacobs maintained a lifelong interest in cities and economics, her books did not center on a single, coherent idea. Instead, she explored a wide range of questions and issues. Yet for all her productivity, *Death and Life* remained her most influential book. Although Jacobs saw herself as a scholar with broad concerns, the public associated her with cities and the opposition to urban renewal in the 1960s.

Significance

While her other books were largely forgotten, *Death and Life* has proved to be a lasting influence. It established Jacobs's reputation as a leading expert on cities, but it also inspired as much as it informed. As the author Anthony Flint writes in his book about Jacobs's battle for a new kind of city regeneration, *Wrestling with Moses*, "The book's influence was undeniable for a new generation of citizen activists, students—who viewed her as a kind of folk hero—and city planners. Activists in cities across the United States modeled themselves after Jacobs, acting as watchdogs over local government and demanding to be heard on everything from street-corner wastebaskets to the shadows cast by proposed skyscrapers."[6]

Death and Life's enduring impact has now lasted more than half a century and its influence has increased over time. In the book, Jacobs predicted the changes cities would undergo after the 1960s. For example, white-collar, gentrifying professionals now find cities desirable places to live for many of the same reasons that Jacobs first outlined. Her ideas are also realized in forms of postmodern architecture* that, starting in the 1980s, became more pervasive (in architecture, "postmodern" refers to a movement that sought to move on from the dominant style of postwar architecture, notably the architectural style known as "modernism"). As the urban theorist David Harvey* wrote, "Architecture and urban design have therefore been presented with new and more wide-ranging opportunities to diversify spatial form than was the case in the immediate postwar period. Dispersed, decentralized, and deconcentrated urban forms are now much more technologically feasible than they once were."[7]

In this way, Jacobs's ideas, which began as a grassroots rallying cry to stay one step ahead of the bulldozer, proved to be ahead of their time as well.

NOTES

1 Jane Jacobs, "Downtown Is for People," *Fortune* (1958), accessed September 6, 2015, http://fortune.com/2011/09/18/downtown-is-for-people-fortune-classic-1958/.

2 Jane Jacobs, *The Economy of Cities* (New York: Random House, 1969), 88–9.

3 Jane Jacobs, *The Question of Separatism: Quebec and the Struggle Over Sovereignty* (New York: Random House, 1980).

4 Jane Jacobs, *Cities and the Wealth of Nations* (New York: Vintage Books, 1984); Jane Jacobs, *Systems of Survival* (New York: Random House, 1992).

5 Jane Jacobs, *The Nature of Economies* (New York: Random House, 2000); Jane Jacobs, *Dark Age Ahead* (New York: Random House, 2004).

6 Anthony Flint, *Wrestling with Moses: How Jane Jacobs Took on New York's Master Builder and Transformed the American City* (New York: Random House, 2009), 185.

7 David Harvey, *The Condition of Postmodernity* (Cambridge, MA: Blackwell, 1990), 75–6.

SECTION 3
IMPACT

MODULE 9
THE FIRST RESPONSES

KEY POINTS

- Jane Jacobs's critics derided her for offering unrealistic alternatives to urban renewal* and ignoring factors such as social class.
- Jacobs did not directly respond to criticism of her ideas but did object to the condescending tone of many of her critics.
- The devastating effects of urban renewal in many cities shaped a consensus that *The Death and Life of Great American Cities* was the right book for its time.

Criticism

Jane Jacobs's *The Death and Life of Great American Cities* received both accolades and criticism following its publication. Writing in the *New York Times* a few months after the book's publication, the notable urban studies* scholar Lloyd Rodwin* offered a dose of both. "Readers will vehemently agree or disagree with the views," Rodwin wrote, "but few of them will go through the volume without looking at their streets and neighborhoods a little differently, a little more sensitively."[1] Indeed, it was impossible to ignore *Death and Life's* originality or the significance of its impact. The editors of *Architectural Forum*,* for whom Jacobs had once written, were even more enthusiastic: "Is it not wonderful whenever long-accepted notions in *any* field are challenged, especially when that challenge is made with high intelligence and on humanistic grounds?"[2] Love it or hate it, *Death and Life* left no doubt that Jane Jacobs had issued a major challenge to the dominant ideas of urban planning.*

One significant critic of *Death and Life* was Lewis Mumford,* a

❝ *Death and Life* never made the bestsellers list, but as soon as it came out, it hit a nerve. Everywhere, people were talking about it, in newspaper editorials and book reviews, in classrooms and boardrooms, and in public symposia. Jacobs had stated her case so forcefully that you couldn't ignore *Death and Life* even if you hated it, as, predictably, many did—especially politicians and developers, and anybody else whose interests she had attacked. ❞

Alice Sparberg Alexiou, *Jane Jacobs: Urban Visionary*

historian of cities who wrote a regular column about architecture for *The New Yorker** magazine. Mumford, who had also opposed some of Robert Moses'* urban renewal projects, encouraged Jacobs after hearing her talk at Harvard's Graduate School of Design and reading her earlier article in *Fortune*, "Downtown Is for People." Yet Jacobs had criticized Mumford's book *The Culture of Cities* in her book, along with prominent urban planners—and Mumford countered with a condescending review of *Death and Life* titled "Mother Jacobs Home Remedies."[3] He dismissed Jacobs as an academic dilettante, an amateur: "I shall say no more of Mrs. Jacobs's lack of historical knowledge and scholarly scruple except that her disregard of easily ascertainable facts is all too frequent."[4]

A more balanced, respectful review came from sociologist Herbert Gans* in *Commentary* magazine. Gans praised *Death and Life* as "a thoughtful and imaginative tract on behalf of the traditional city."[5] But he also took issue with what he called Jacobs's "physical fallacy," which led her to "ignore the social, cultural, and economic factors that contribute to vitality or dullness."[6] In brief, Jacobs's analysis failed to consider additional variables such as social class. "In proposing that cities be planned to stimulate an abundant street life," he continued, "Jacobs not only overestimates the power of planning in shaping behavior, but she in effect demands that middle-class people adopt working-class styles of family life, child rearing, and sociability."[7] Gans argued that this perspective limited the scope of her analysis.

Responses

For the most part, Jacobs did not directly reply to her critics; but she continued to take part in activism against urban renewal, a strong indication that she was willing to stand by her argument. Jacobs further developed many of the ideas initially laid out in *Death and Life* in her second book, *The Economy of Cities*.

More than four decades after *Death and Life*'s publication, Jacobs recounted her feelings about Mumford's review in a 2004 lecture at City College in New York. She ridiculed Mumford's smug sexism, which other critics also employed: "I thought his reaction to the book was not quite rational … Maybe if he'd lived at a different time he would have understood that women didn't necessarily aspire to be patronized. He believed that women were a sort of ladies' auxiliary of the human race."[8]

Still, Jacobs seemed hurt by her more thoughtful and less politically motivated critics. Her biographer noted that "she often does not take criticism well."[9] In particular, she was "very angry" with Herbert Gans's review in *Commentary*, which balanced praise and criticism.[10] Jacobs and Gans had previously met and exchanged ideas when she was in Boston, and in 1962 Gans focused in his own book, *The Urban Villagers*, on the struggle with urban renewal experienced by Boston's North End neighborhood.[11]

Conflict and Consensus

The general consensus among Jacobs's critics was that she correctly identified the negative impact of urban renewal. Indeed, its devastating effects were evident in any number of cities across the country. Yet many also agreed that her solutions and suggestions were misguided or simply wrong. In short, many held that "it was Jacobs's analysis that made her book brilliant, but not her prescriptions."[12] As Gans pointed out in his review of *Death and Life*, most middle-class people did not necessarily desire diversity, were more drawn to suburban neighborhoods than to urban ones, and were not eager to walk or use public transportation.[13]

Over time, debates about *Death and Life* shifted in focus. As American politics took a turn to the right, some leftist critics observed that conservatives could appropriate her ideas. In 1982, the political scientist Marshall Berman* wrote, "What is relevant and disturbing here is that ideologues of the New Right have more than once cited Jacobs as one of their patron saints ... It seems to me that beneath her modernist text there is an anti-modernist subtext, a sort of undertow of nostalgia for a family and a neighborhood in which the self could be securely embedded."[14]

The nostalgic strain of *Death and Life* began to mesh with conservative values and sentimentality in the 1980s. This had not necessarily been Jacobs's intent, but the shifting social context produced some apparent common ground—unusually, since conservatives of Jacobs's time would hardly have considered themselves defenders of the city.

NOTES

1   Lloyd Rodwin, "Neighbors Are Needed," *New York Times*, November 5, 1961.

2   Quoted in Alice Sparberg Alexiou, *Jane Jacobs: Urban Visionary* (New Brunswick, NJ: Rutgers University Press, 2006), 84.

3   Lewis Mumford, "The Sky Line: 'Mother Jacobs Home Remedies,'" *The New Yorker*, December 1, 1962.

4   Mumford, "The Sky Line."

5   Herbert Gans, "City Planning and Urban Realities," *Commentary* 33 (February 1962): 170–5.

6   Gans, "City Planning and Urban Realities."

7   Gans, "City Planning and Urban Realities."

8   Quoted in Alexiou, *Jane Jacobs*, 94.

9   Alexiou, *Jane Jacobs*, 94.

10 Alexiou, *Jane Jacobs*, 94.

11 Herbert Gans, *The Urban Villagers: Group and Class in the Life of Italian-Americans* (New York: Free Press of Glencoe, 1962).

12 Alexiou, *Jane Jacobs*, 83.

13 Gans, "City Planning and Urban Realities."

14 Marshall Berman, *All That Is Solid Melts into Air: The Experience of Modernity* (New York: Penguin Books, 1982), 320.

MODULE 10
THE EVOLVING DEBATE

KEY POINTS

- Jane Jacobs's ideas gave new relevance to the study of gentrification—a process in which a neighborhood is regenerated so successfully that its original residents can no longer afford it—and influenced alternative forms of urban planning.*

- The New Urbanism* school of thought was inspired in part by *The Death and Life of American Cities*.

- Jacobs's ideas were transformative for urban studies* and many of its leading scholars, such as Richard Sennett* and Sharon Zukin.*

Uses and Problems

In *The Death and Life of Great American Cities* Jane Jacobs attacked ideas of urban planning that had been dominant since the end of World War II.* By the time of the book's publication in 1961, the urban renewal* projects of planners such as Robert Moses* were coming to an end. Cities faced an era of change, and Jacobs's ideas both indicated and catalyzed those changes. The first signs of gentrification had begun to appear, transforming many urban neighborhoods by the 1980s. In retrospect, Jacobs's ideas acquired renewed importance as a portent of those changes: "Gentrification was the central tension in her work, but in 1961 Jacobs did not yet have the vocabulary to make sense of it. Her Hudson Street in reality was not a quaint village but a dynamic middle ground lodged fragilely between an expanding postindustrial landscape and a declining industrial one."[1]

At the leading edge of gentrification were young middle-class

❝ If writers like Jane Jacobs sought to rescue place from modern capitalist assimilation, they also commemorated a specific locale in the metropolis at a fleeting moment in the city's evolution: a nineteenth-century industrial middle cityscape on the periphery of the postwar modern central business district or university campus, in the early stages of gentrification.* **❞**

Suleiman Osman, *The Invention of Brownstone Brooklyn*

professionals in search of an authentic feel and lifestyle they could not find in the suburbs. They associated this with the ethnic communities, local businesses, aged buildings, and walkable streets that Jacobs described in *Death and Life*. As the urban sociologist and leading theorist of gentrification Sharon Zukin put it, "Jane Jacobs expressed the appeal of this new sense of urban authenticity better than anyone."[2] *Death and Life* has taken on new significance as urban theorists seek to understand gentrification—and the white-collar quest for the authentic that fuels it.

Schools of Thought

Jacobs became one of the most important influences in the rise of the design and planning movement known as New Urbanism. This loosely defined group includes architects, planners, and scholars who advocate planning diversity, stress the importance of street life, and offer specific architectural solutions to address these goals.[3] Their core principles were laid out in a 1993 charter: "The Congress for the New Urbanism views disinvestment in central cities, the spread of placeless sprawl, increasing separation by race and income, environmental deterioration, loss of agricultural lands and wilderness, and the erosion of society's built heritage as one interrelated community-building challenge."[4]

New Urbanism built on Jacobs's ideas and applied them to the contemporary problems of social inequality and ecological peril.

Since the 1990s, New Urbanism has attracted many practitioners and has become one of the most influential movements in urban planning. Its adherents have also incited no shortage of criticism. For example, the urban theorist David Harvey*—a scholar who addresses the relationship between capitalism and social space, an approach typical of those who draw on the theoretical tools provided by Marxist* analysis of society and economics—accused the New Urbanists of mainly addressing the needs of young middle-class professionals, while ignoring the plight of the inner city's underclass.[5] Others have criticized New Urbanism's disciples because they apply their ideas to smaller cities, planned communities, and neighborhoods not integrated into the metropolis; some also argue that their projects feel artificial and too strictly planned.[6]

Jacobs herself seemed to echo these criticisms when she was asked about New Urbanism in a 2001 interview: "The New Urbanists want to have lively centers in the places that they develop, where people run into each other doing errands and that sort of thing. And yet, from what I've seen of their plans and the places they have built, they don't seem to have a sense of the anatomy of these hearts, these centers. They've placed them as if they were shopping centers. They don't connect."[7] Thus, although Jacobs clearly inspired the New Urbanists, she maintained that they misinterpreted her ideas.

In Current Scholarship

Jacobs's *Death and Life* has impacted many contemporary scholars and practitioners of urban design and planning. Jacobs has influenced two leading American urbanists, Richard Sennett and Sharon Zukin, though they also maintain a critical distance from some of her ideas. Sennett is interested in how people experience cities through their bodily senses. He uses methods similar to Jacobs's to examine everyday life and social interaction in Greenwich Village. "Like so many others," Sennett wrote, "I had read my way into Greenwich Village, before arriving there twenty years ago, in the pages of Jane Jacobs's *The Death and Life of Great American Cities*."[8] While Sennett ultimately disagreed with many of Jacobs's conclusions, his intellectual debt to her is clear.

Sharon Zukin is another scholar indebted to Jacobs, even though she also diverged from her ideas. In her studies of gentrification, Zukin further developed some of Jacobs's ideas about the intersections of cities and culture. She has also examined issues Jacobs neglected, especially questions of race, class, and social inequality in the city. Yet while Zukin differentiated herself from Jacobs, she recognized that *Death and Life* had continuing relevance for the study of gentrification, and in fact had anticipated this change: "She connected small, old buildings and cheap rents with neighborhood street life, specialized, low-price shops, and new, interesting economic activities: in other words, downtown's social values."[9]

NOTES

1   Suleiman Osman, *The Invention of Brownstone Brooklyn: Gentrification and the Search for Authenticity in Postwar New York* (New York: Oxford University Press, 2011), 177.

2   Sharon Zukin, *Naked City: The Death and Life of Authentic Urban Spaces* (New York: Oxford University Press, 2010), 16.

3   Peter Katz, *The New Urbanism: Toward an Architecture of Community* (New York: McGraw-Hill, 1994).

4   Congress for the New Urbanism, "Charter of the New Urbanism," in *The City Reader*, 5th edn, ed. Richard T. LeGates and Frederic Stout (New York: Routledge, 2011), 357.

5   David Harvey, "The New Urbanism and the Communitarian Trap," *Harvard Design Magazine* 1 (1997): 68–9.

6   See Todd W. Bressi, ed., *The Seaside Debates: A Critique of the New Urbanism* (New York: Rizzoli, 2002).

7   Jane Jacobs and Bill Steigerwald, "City Views: Urban Studies Legend Jane

Jacobs on Gentrification, the New Urbanism, and Her Legacy," Reason 33, no. 2 (June 2001).

8   Richard Sennett, *Flesh and Stone: The Body and the City in Western Civilization* (New York: W. W. Norton, 1994), 355.

9   Sharon Zukin, *Landscapes of Power: From Detroit to Disney World* (Berkeley and Los Angeles: University of California Press, 1991), 191.

MODULE 11
IMPACT AND INFLUENCE TODAY

KEY POINTS

- *The Death and Life of Great American Cities* is widely considered a classic work of urban studies* and urban planning.*

- *Death and Life* continues to challenge urban planners to build cities that improve the quality of life for their inhabitants.

- The debates continue between theorists and planners concerning the rightful heirs to Jacobs's ideas.

Position

Jane Jacobs's *The Death and Life of Great American Cities* is indisputably an urban studies classic. The general consensus is that the book transformed approaches to the city in both theory and practice. *Death and Life* opened new theoretical debates about the function of cities in postwar America and abroad, and marked a significant change in how cities were designed and planned. Jacobs's book regularly appears on reading lists for courses in a broad array of disciplines and is often reprinted in excerpts for edited anthologies about cities;[1] and it is almost always discussed in urban studies textbooks.[2]

In the decades since *Death and Life*'s publication, critiques have shifted from institutional questions about urban renewal* to Jacobs's neglect of issues such as race, class, and social inequality. The sociologist Sharon Zukin* and the Marxist* geographer David Harvey* have stood at the forefront of this changing focus. Jacobs was initially criticized for her lack of academic qualifications, absence of a systematic methodology, and oversimplification of the literature.[3]

❝ The girl from Scranton stood up to Moses* and challenged the status quo. Now virtually all those engaged in city building follow her rules. Her triumphs are engraved in the protocols followed by developers, city officials, and advocacy and grassroots organizations, and copies of *The Death and Life of Great American Cities* sit on the shelves of the planning offices at city halls across the country. ❞

Anthony Flint, *Wrestling with Moses: How Jane Jacobs Took on New York's Master Builder and Transformed the American City*

However, these objections are now seen as less important, whereas her disregard of race and class poses more problems. Her idealization of Greenwich Village, for example, lacks any analysis of inequality: "This is what makes her neighborhood vision seem pastoral: it is the city before the blacks got there. Her world ranges from solid working-class whites at the bottom to professional middle-class whites at the top."[4] So while *Death and Life* is still considered a classic, scholars interested in race and class must look elsewhere.

Interaction

Jacobs wrote *Death and Life* in a historical context in which urban renewal was ravaging cities, and where a litany of faulty assumptions shaped the approach of planners. When Jacobs challenged this orthodoxy,* it lost its unquestioned power. Since then, many of the core ideas of *Death and Life* have become the new common sense of urban design and planning. Therefore, as the debates within urban studies have long since moved on, *Death and Life*'s critique of city planning has become canonical.

One group of theorists and planners who have inherited and extended Jacobs's ideas, including Richard Sennett* and the urban studies professor Richard Burdett* of the London School of Economics, advocate for an "open city"*—a city based on principles of democracy and diversity. Sennett's use of Jacobs follows the spirit and intent of *Death and Life*; he invokes Jacobs in explaining the open-city idea. He argues that Jacobs "believes that in an open city, as in the natural world, social and visual forms mutate through chance variation; people can best absorb, participate, and adapt to change" in what he calls "urban time."[5]

New Urbanism* is composed of a second group of theorists and planners whom Jacobs influenced. In their planned communities, the New Urbanists have incorporated many of Jacobs's suggestions for mixed-use districts,* short blocks, and pedestrian-friendly neighborhoods. These core principles are outlined in their founding charter: "Neighborhoods should be diverse in use and population; communities should be designed for the pedestrian and transit as well as the car; cities and towns should be shaped by physically defined and universally accessible public spaces and community institutions; urban places should be framed by architecture and landscape design that celebrate local history, climate, ecology, and building practice."[6]

Although Jacobs distanced herself from New Urbanism,[7] *Death and Life* is clearly a foundational text for its ideas.

The Continuing Debate

Jacobs has become a venerated figure in urban studies. Yet while numerous theorists and planners claim her as an influence, some points of debate remain. One contemporary scholar who challenges Jacobs and her disciplines is the Harvard economist Edward Glaeser.* In his book *Triumph of the City*, Glaeser declares, "Many of the ideas in this book draw on the wisdom of Jane Jacobs, who knew that you need to walk a city's streets to see its soul."[8] Nevertheless, Glaeser proceeds to argue against some of Jacobs's conclusions on theoretical and methodological grounds. Jacobs, he maintains, "also made mistakes that came from relying too much on her ground-level view and not using conceptual tools that help one think through an entire system."[9] Specifically, Glaeser challenges her conclusion that restricting the height of buildings and preserving older neighborhoods would make cities more affordable—and suggests that planners should revisit the benefits of high-rise apartments and skyscrapers.

Like advocates of the open city and New Urbanists, Glaeser is concerned with the environmental impact of urban living, but less troubled by its social inequalities. The varying responses to Jacobs are partly a result of the different ways of putting her ideas into practice. Glaeser is an urban economist who examines cities as a scholar and theorist; the New Urbanists, by contrast, are mostly practitioners who embody her notions in planned communities and architecture. Glaeser claims to work in the tradition of Jacobs, as do the advocates of the open city and the planners who practice New Urbanism—but to be sure, the conclusions each of these disciples reach are very different.

NOTES

1   See Richard T. LeGates and Frederic Stout, eds, *The City Reader*, 5th edn (New York: Routledge, 2011); Janet Lin and Christopher Mele, eds, *The Urban Sociology Reader*, 2nd edn (New York: Routledge, 2012).

2   See Mark Gottdiener, Ray Hutchison, and Michael T. Ryan, *The New Urban Sociology*, 5th edn (Boulder, CO: Westview Press, 2015); John J. Macionis and Vincent M. Parrillo, *Cities and Urban Life*, 6th edn (Boston, MA: Pearson, 2013).

3   See Lewis Mumford, "The Sky Line: 'Mother Jacobs Home Remedies,'" *The New Yorker*, December 1, 1962.

4   Marshall Berman, *All That Is Solid Melts into Air: The Experience of Modernity* (New York: Penguin Books, 1982), 324.

5   Richard Sennett, "The Open City," *Urban Age* (2006): 2–3.

6   Congress for the New Urbanism, "Charter of the New Urbanism," in *The City Reader*, 5th edn, ed. Richard T. LeGates and Frederic Stout (New York: Routledge, 2011), 357.

7   Jane Jacobs and Bill Steigerwald, "City Views: Urban Studies Legend Jane
     Jacobs on Gentrification, the New Urbanism, and Her Legacy," *Reason* 33,
     no. 2 (2001): 48–55.

8   Edward Glaeser, *Triumph of the City: How Our Greatest Invention Makes Us
     Richer, Smarter, Greener, Healthier, and Happier* (New York: Penguin Press,
     2011), 11.

9   Glaeser, *Triumph of the City*, 11.

MODULE 12
WHERE NEXT?

KEY POINTS

- As the populations of cities around the world continue to increase, *The Death and Life of American Cities* is likely to grow in influence.

- *Death and Life* will continue to serve as a foundational text for theories of urban planning* that supplanted the ideas and practices typical of the years following World War II.*

- *Death and Life* was a groundbreaking work in its critique of urban renewal,* its description of social interaction in cities, and its foreshadowing of gentrification.*

Potential

Jane Jacobs's *The Death and Life of Great American Cities* could be about to exert its influence on theorists and planners outside the United States. As of 2015, a majority of the world's people live in urban areas—a first in global history.[1] Cities around the world are growing faster than ever before, with no end in sight. The United Nations estimates that if growth continues at the current rate, the world's urban population will double every 38 years.[2] Clearly, these conditions demand a sharper understanding of what makes cities work and how to plan them, and this is where Jacobs's book could be influential.

Global cities can benefit from incorporating Jane Jacobs's insights about the relationship between economics and space. Contemporary urban theorists such as Richard Florida* emphasize the importance of cities for economic innovation.[3] Florida and many others—including those outside the academic realm—recognize that urban spaces play a crucial role in nurturing the creativity and diversity needed to compete

❝ But in some places, such as Argentina, where a Spanish translation of one of her works lay deep in the stacks of the one library that owned it, Jane Jacobs is only now getting a following, as a nascent preservation movement in creatively destructive Buenos Aires seeks a philosophic grounding ... In all these places, we are reminded that Jane Jacobs remains, 50 years after Death and Life, an important figure whose influence continues to evolve. **❞**

Max Page and Timothy Mennel, *Reconsidering Jane Jacobs*

in a global economy. As Malcolm Gladwell,* the author of several books on social science, wrote in 2000, "To reread *Death and Life* today is to be struck by how the intervening years have given her arguments a new and unexpected relevance. Who, after all, has a direct interest in creating diverse, vital spaces that foster creativity and serendipity? Employers do. On the fortieth anniversary of its publication, *Death and Life* has been reborn as a primer on workplace design."[4]

Future Directions

The main group of theorists and planners carrying out Jacobs's ideas and applying her prescriptions call themselves New Urbanists.*[5] In sum, "New Urbanists, who regard *Death and Life* as the most important initial theoretical contribution to their movement, not only rely on Jacobs's concepts of city density, walkable communities and 'street eyes,' but also on her belief in the mix of uses, buildings and people."[6] The New Urbanists have implemented many of Jacobs's suggestions in their plans and designs, particularly those that foster social interaction and a diversity of uses.

However, Jacobs distanced herself from this movement in a 2001 interview.[7] Some theorists and planners have criticized New Urbanism for taking Jacobs's ideas out of an urban context and applying them to communities more like suburbs or small towns:[8] "The main problem in the application of Jacobs' ideas to New Urbanism revolves around the question of whether diversity can be planned as theories in planning and urban design postulate."[9]

The irony is that whereas Jacobs criticized the urban planning of her time and advocated a more organic, spontaneous approach to cities, her ideas now find expression in new forms of planning within smaller non-urban communities. Although they may not be urban in character, they at least attempt to reflect Jacobs's ideas.

Summary

Death and Life fundamentally changed urban studies* and urban planning, and its impact continues. When it was published in 1961, a neighborhood movement in Greenwich Village, involving Jacobs herself, fought the urban renewal* projects of the architect and planner Robert Moses.* These events shaped *Death and Life*, and the movement's success validated the book's objections to urban renewal. In debunking the orthodox* theories implemented by Moses and other planners, Jacobs offered an alternative set of ideas about how cities work by fostering social interaction. Her suggestions for mixed-use* spaces, walkable neighborhoods, and historical preservation* have since been widely accepted in urban planning.

The historical significance and wide-ranging impact of *Death and Life* make it an indispensable work in urban studies and planning. It has since become a foundational text for contemporary theories and planners, such as those associated with New Urbanism. Even when scholars such as Edward Glaeser* respectfully disagree with Jacobs's ideas, *Death and Life* continues to be a major touchstone in the field.[10] Her analysis of Greenwich Village also anticipated the onset of gentrification that has transformed numerous city neighborhoods in the decades since *Death and Life* was published. Scholars including the sociologist* Sharon Zukin* have argued that Jacobs neglected the inequalities of race and class that have come to the fore with gentrification, but here again Jacobs's ability to connect cities and culture was groundbreaking.[11]

The political scientist Marshall Berman* wrote that Jacobs described the "modernism of the street" in *Death and Life*.[12] What he meant was that she captured the excitement, creativity, and dynamism generated by the mixture of people in an urban environment. Her vision represented the antithesis of that held by planners such as Moses, who sought to destroy cities because they feared the streets and dense concentrations of people. However, those fears proved unfounded, and as Jacobs's ideas gained favor, the projects championed by Moses and his ilk bit the dust before they ever got off the ground. And more than 50 years after Jacobs and Moses locked horns in a Greenwich Village showdown, cities are here to stay. As they continue to grow, so too, it appears, will Jacobs's influence.

NOTES

1 Mark Gottdiener, Ray Hutchison, and Michael T. Ryan, *The New Urban Sociology*, 5th edn (Boulder, CO: Westview Press, 2015), 9.

2 Gottdiener, Hutchison, and Ryan, *The New Urban Sociology*, 10.

3 Richard Florida, *The Rise of the Creative Class* (New York: Basic Books, 2002).

4 Malcolm Gladwell, "Designs for Working," *The New Yorker*, December 11, 2000.

5 Peter Katz, *The New Urbanism: Towards an Architecture of Community* (New York: McGraw-Hill, 1994).

6 Matthias Wendt, "The Importance of *Death and Life of Great American Cities* by Jane Jacobs to the Profession of Urban Planning," *New Visions for Public Affairs* 1 (Spring 2009).

7 Jane Jacobs and Bill Steigerwald, "City Views: Urban Studies Legend Jane Jacobs on Gentrification, the New Urbanism, and Her Legacy," *Reason* 33, no. 2 (2001): 48–55.

8   See Max Page and Timothy Mennel, eds, *Reconsidering Jane Jacobs* (Chicago: American Planning Association, 2011).

9   Wendt, "The Importance of *Death and Life of Great American Cities*."

10   Edward Glaeser, *Triumph of the City: How Our Greatest Invention Makes Us Richer, Smarter, Greener, Healthier, and Happier* (New York: Penguin Press, 2011).

11   Sharon Zukin, *Naked City: The Death and Life of Authentic Urban Spaces* (New York: Oxford University Press, 2010).

12   Marshall Berman, *All That Is Solid Melts into Air: The Experience of Modernity* (New York: Penguin Books, 1982), 314.

GLOSSARY

GLOSSARY OF TERMS

Architectural Forum: an American magazine of architecture and home design published from 1892 to 1974.

Chicago School: best known for its urban sociology, this was a faculty in the sociology department at the University of Chicago that produced groundbreaking studies of urban life during the 1920s and 1930s. Chicago sociologists undertook many ethnographic studies of urban subcultures and lifestyles, and their theories compared social life in the city to an ecological system.

Cross Bronx Expressway: a major highway for automobiles designed by Robert Moses and built between 1948 and 1972. Its construction entailed the demolition of thousands of homes and business in the southern part of the Bronx, with destructive long-term consequences for its neighborhoods.

Decentrists: a group of urban theorists and planners from the nineteenth century who sought to reform the social and environmental ills of city life by decentralizing the population and built environment of cities.

Garden city: a utopian ideal of urban planning developed by Ebenezer Howard in the late nineteenth century as an alternative to the densely populated cities of the time. Its design was supposed to combine the best features of city and country living.

Gentrification: the migration of white-collar (middle-class) professionals to formerly deteriorated urban neighborhoods. It increases property values and housing costs, displacing its previous low-income inhabitants, and incorporates the cultural tastes of white-collar workers for food, art, music, and recreation.

Greenwich Village: a neighborhood in Lower Manhattan that developed a reputation as a bohemian, free-thinking haven for writers, artists, musicians, and political dissidents.

Historical preservation: a movement to protect, preserve, and restore buildings, monuments, and objects with historic significance in urban areas. This movement was energized by community opposition to the demolition projects of urban renewal.

Joint Committee to Stop the Lower Manhattan Expressway: a local movement that succeeded in stopping the construction of an automotive expressway designed by Robert Moses to cut through the neighborhoods and business districts of Lower Manhattan.

Lower Manhattan Expressway: the plan proposed by the planner Robert Moses to build an automotive expressway that would connect the eastern and western ends of Lower Manhattan. The project would have entailed the demolition of the neighborhoods now known as SoHo and Little Italy. Community opposition forced the project's cancellation in 1962.

Marxism: both a methodology for sociological analysis and a theory of historical development. Inspired by the writings of the German economist and political philosopher Karl Marx, its traditional emphasis has been on class conflict and the economic determination of behavior, and on providing a systemic and incisive critique of the capitalist (that is, profit-oriented) economy.

Mixed-use development: districts or zones that blend a combination of industrial, commercial, residential, and cultural spaces. The benefits of this combination include reduced distances between destinations, stronger neighborhood character, and more bicycle- and pedestrian-friendly streets. Mixed-use districts are increasingly associated with gentrification.

New Urbanism: a movement in urban design and planning that arose in the 1980s and 1990s. New Urbanists have designed numerous neighborhoods that incorporate walkable streets, downtown centers, historical preservation, and environmental sustainability.

Open city: an urban ideal for a city based on principles of democracy and diversity proposed by the urban scholars Richard Burdett and Richard Sennett of the London School of Economics. Its key features are passage territories, incomplete form, narratives of development, and democratic space.

Orthodox: something that conforms to traditional or generally accepted rules or practice.

Orthodoxy: a generally accepted theory, doctrine, or practice.

Postmodern architecture: a movement starting in the late 1970s involving architects who sought to move on from the International Style that dominated postwar architecture. In contrast to architectural modernism, it incorporates self-referential wit and non-functional ornamentation.

Radiant City: the architect Le Corbusier's model of an ideal city, developed in the 1920s and 1930s. This ideal city would be composed of high-rise buildings, efficient flows of traffic, and abundant green spaces.

Second-wave feminism: the social movement of women that began in the late 1960s, continuing earlier movements of women for suffrage, nondiscrimination, reproductive rights, and social equality.

Sociology: the study of the history, formation, and structures of human societies.

Spadina Expressway: a proposed freeway that would have run through downtown Toronto. The project was canceled in 1971 as a result of public opposition.

The New Yorker: a weekly magazine published since 1925 that includes fiction, journalism, poetry, criticism, satire, and cartoons.

Urban planning: the technical process of designing cities with concerns for infrastructure, transportation, communications, and public welfare.

Urban renewal: projects of reconstruction that were most often implemented in cities after World War II. Urban renewal typically involved the demolition of inner-city neighborhoods for the construction of automotive highways.

Urban sociology: the study of the social constitution of urban environments.

Urban studies: an academic field that combines multiple disciplines for the study of cities and their suburbs. Its most common subtopics include urban economics, urban planning, urban politics, urban transportation, and urban sociology.

Washington Square Park: a public square and gathering place central to the neighborhood of Greenwich Village in New York City. Since the late nineteenth century, this park has been a vital spot for congregating and performing for musicians, artists, poets, and entertainers.

Washington Square Park Committee: a group founded by Shirley Hayes in 1952 to halt New York City's plans to extend automobile traffic through Washington Square Park in Greenwich Village.

World War II: global conflict from 1939 to 1945 that involved the world's great powers and numerous other countries around the globe.

PEOPLE MENTIONED IN THE TEXT

Jane Addams (1860–1935) was a social reformer and the co-founder of Hull House, a social reform center in Chicago. Her social work increased awareness of the problems of poverty and public health in cities.

Marshall Berman (1940–2013) was Distinguished Professor of Political Science at the City College of New York and the Graduate Center of the City University of New York. He was best known for his analysis of modernity from a Marxist humanist perspective.

Richard Burdett is professor of urban studies at the London School of Economics. He has played a central role in developing the idea of an "open city."

Ernest Burgess (1886–1966) was an urban sociologist at the University of Chicago. He is most noted for his theory of how cities grow in concentric zones.

Rachel Carson (1907–1964) was a marine biologist and conservationist. Her book *Silent Spring* exposed the harmful effects of pesticide use and influenced the beginnings of the environmental movement.

Richard Florida (b. 1957) is an urban theorist and professor at the Rotman School of Management at the University of Toronto. He is best known for his writings about how cities can stimulate the economic innovation of a "creative class."

Betty Friedan (1921–2006) was a feminist writer as well as the co-founder and first president of the National Organization of Women (NOW). Her book *The Feminine Mystique* is often credited with being a catalyst for the development of second-wave feminism in the 1960s.

Herbert Gans (b. 1927) is a sociologist who taught at Columbia University between 1971 and 2007. His work has spanned a wide range of topics, including the effects of urban renewal, the lives of the poor, and the workings of the news media.

Sir Patrick Geddes (1854–1932) was a Scottish intellectual and a pioneering figure in urban planning. He developed ideas for regional planning that opposed the gridiron plans that dominated cities in his time.

Malcolm Gladwell (b. 1963) is a journalist and has been a staff writer at *The New Yorker* magazine since 1996. His five books exploring the surprising implications of academic social science have all been *New York Times* bestsellers.

Edward Glaeser (b. 1967) is professor of economics at Harvard University. His research examines how cities foster economic prosperity and environmental sustainability.

Michael Harrington (1928–1989) was a writer and founder of the Democratic Socialists of America. His first book, *The Other America*, helped launch the War on Poverty in the United States during the 1960s.

David Harvey (b. 1935) is Distinguished Professor of Anthropology and Geography at the City University of New York. He is known for his Marxist analysis of the relationship between capitalism and social space.

Shirley Hayes (1912–2002) was a community organizer in New York's Greenwich Village. She founded the Washington Square Park Committee to combat Robert Moses' plans to build expressways across Lower Manhattan.

Ebenezer Howard (1850–1928) was an English theorist of urban planning. He envisioned and designed a garden city based on utopian ideas that combined the best aspects of city and country living.

Le Corbusier (1887–1965) was a Swiss French architect and urban planner. His architectural ideas informed the redesign of Paris in the 1920s and 1930s, and his buildings can be found in many parts of the world.

Robert Moses (1888–1981) was an urban planner and public official who held numerous positions in New York City between 1922 and 1968. He is known as the "master builder" who transformed New York and its surrounding suburbs in the mid-twentieth century.

Lewis Mumford (1895–1990) was an American writer on cities and the architecture critic for *The New Yorker* magazine. He is best known for his book *The City in History*, which won the National Book Award for Nonfiction in 1962.

Ralph Nader (b. 1932) is a consumer advocate, environmental activist, and humanitarian. From 1992 to 2008, he was a candidate for president of the United States five times.

Robert Park (1864–1944) was an urban sociologist who taught at the University of Chicago from 1914 to 1933. His work examined issues of urban ecology, social disorganization, race relations, migration, and assimilation.

Lloyd Rodwin (1919–1999) was professor of urban studies at the Massachusetts Institute of Technology (MIT) and co-founder of the MIT–Harvard Joint Center for Urban Studies. He wrote 11 books and played an important role in urban planning during the 1950s and 1960s.

Saskia Sassen (b. 1947) is a professor of sociology at Columbia University. She has been a pioneering figure in studies of globalization and cities, with her books being translated into 21 languages.

Richard Sennett (b. 1943) is Emeritus Professor of Sociology at the London School of Economics. He has written numerous books about the development of cities, social class, public culture, and work in modern society.

William H. Whyte (1917–1999) was a sociologist, urbanist, and organizational analyst. He is best known for his 1956 book *The Organization Man*, which sold more than two million copies.

Louis Wirth (1897–1952) was a sociologist at the University of Chicago and a leading figure in the Chicago School. He is best known for his work on urbanism as a way of life in cities.

Sharon Zukin is professor of sociology at Brooklyn College and at the Graduate Center of the City University of New York. Her books have examined gentrification and the relationship between cities and culture, primarily in New York.

WORKS CITED

WORKS CITED

Alexiou, Alice Sparberg. *Jane Jacobs: Urban Visionary*. New Brunswick, NJ: Rutgers University Press, 2006.

Berman, Marshall. *All That Is Solid Melts into Air: The Experience of Modernity*. New York: Penguin Books, 1982.

Bressi, Todd W., ed. *The Seaside Debates: A Critique of the New Urbanism*. New York: Rizzoli, 2002.

Carson, Rachel. *Silent Spring*. Boston: Houghton Mifflin Company, 1962.

Congress for the New Urbanism. "Charter of the New Urbanism." In *The City Reader*, edited by Richard T. LeGates and Frederic Stout, 356–9. New York: Routledge, 2011.

Dreier, Peter. "Jane Jacobs' Radical Legacy." *National Housing Institute* 146 (Summer 2006). Accessed September 5, 2015. http://www.nhi.org/online/issues/146/janejacobslegacy.html.

Flint, Anthony. *Wrestling with Moses: How Jane Jacobs Took on New York's Master Builder and Transformed the American City*. New York: Random House, 2009.

Florida, Richard. *The Rise of the Creative Class*. New York: Basic Books, 2002.

Friedan, Betty. *The Feminine Mystique*. New York: W. W. Norton, 1963.

Gans, Herbert. "City Planning and Urban Realities." *Commentary* 33 (February 1962): 170–5.

———. *The Urban Villagers: Group and Class in the Life of Italian Americans*. New York: Free Press of Glencoe, 1962.

Gladwell, Malcolm. "Designs for Working." *The New Yorker,* December 11, 2000.

Glaeser, Edward. *Triumph of the City: How Our Greatest Invention Makes Us Richer, Smarter, Greener, Healthier, and Happier*. New York: Penguin Press, 2011.

Gottdiener, Mark, Ray Hutchinson, and Michael T. Ryan. *The New Urban Sociology*. Boulder, CO: Westview Press, 2015.

Gratz, Roberta Brandes. *The Battle for Gotham: New York in the Shadow of Robert Moses and Jane Jacobs*. New York: Nation Books, 2010.

Harrington, Michael. *The Other America: Poverty in the United States*. New York: Touchstone, 1962.

Harvey, David. *The Condition of Postmodernity*. Cambridge, MA: Blackwell, 1990.

———. "The New Urbanism and the Communitarian Trap." *Harvard Design Magazine* 1 (1997): 68–9.

Jacobs, Jane. "Downtown Is for People," *Fortune* 57 (April 1958): 157–84. Accessed September 6, 2015. http://fortune.com/2011/09/18/downtown-is-for-people-fortune-classic-1958/.

———. *The Economy of Cities*. New York: Random House, 1969.

———. *The Question of Separatism: Quebec and the Struggle Over Sovereignty*. New York: Random House, 1980.

———. *Cities and the Wealth of Nations*. New York: Vintage Books, 1984.

———. *The Death and Life of Great American Cities*. New York: Vintage Books, 1992.

———. *Systems of Survival*. New York: Random House, 1992.

———. *The Nature of Economies*. New York: Random House, 2000.

———. *Dark Age Ahead*. New York: Random House, 2004.

Jacobs, Jane, and Bill Steigerwald, "City Views: Urban Studies Legend Jane Jacobs on Gentrification, the New Urbanism, and Her Legacy," *Reason* 33, no. 2 (June 2001). Accessed September 13, 2015. https://reason.com/archives/2001/06/01/city-views.

Katz, Peter. *The New Urbanism: Toward an Architecture of Community*. New York: McGraw-Hill, 1994.

Kidd, Kenneth. "Did Jane Jacobs's Critics Have a Point After All?" *The Toronto Star*, November 25, 2011. Accessed August 31, 2015. http://www.thestar.com/news/insight/2011/11/25/did_jane_jacobs_critics_have_a_point_after_all.html.

LeGates, Richard T., and Frederic Stout, eds. *The City Reader*. New York: Routledge, 2011.

Lin, Janet, and Christopher Mele, eds. *The Urban Sociology Reader*. New York: Routledge, 2012.

Macionis, John J., and Vincent M. Parrillo, *Cities and Urban Life*. Boston: Pearson, 2013.

Mumford, Lewis. "The Sky Line: 'Mother Jacobs Home Remedies.'" *The New Yorker*, December 1, 1962.

Nader, Ralph. *Unsafe at Any Speed: The Designed-In Dangers of the American Automobile*. New York: Grossman, 1965.

Osman, Suleiman. *The Invention of Brownstone Brooklyn: Gentrification and the Search for Authenticity in Postwar New York*. New York: Oxford University Press, 2011.

Page, Max, and Timothy Mennel, eds. *Reconsidering Jane Jacobs*. Chicago: American Planning Association, 2011.

Rodwin, Lloyd. "Neighbors Are Needed." *New York Times*, November 5, 1961.

Sassen, Saskia. "What Would Jane Jacobs See in the Global City? Place and Social Practices." In *The Urban Wisdom of Jane Jacobs*, edited by Sonia Hirt and Diana Zahm, 84–99. New York: Routledge, 2012.

Sennett, Richard. *Flesh and Stone: The Body and the City in Western Civilization*. New York: W. W. Norton, 1994.

———. "The Open City." *Urban Age* (November 2006): 2–3.

Strausbaugh, John. *The Village: A History of Greenwich Village*. New York: HarperCollins, 2013.

Ward, Stephen. "Obituary: Jane Jacobs." *The Independent*, June 3, 2006. Accessed August 29, 2015. http://www.independent.co.uk/news/obituaries/jane-jacobs-6099183.html.

Wendt, Matthias. "The Importance of *Death and Life of Great American Cities* by Jane Jacobs to the Profession of Urban Planning," *New Visions for Public Affairs* 1 (Spring 2009). Accessed September 13, 2015. https://nvpajournal.wordpress.com/issues/volume-1/.

Wirth, Louis. "Urbanism as a Way of Life." *American Journal of Sociology* 44, no. 1 (July 1938): 1–24.

Zukin, Sharon. *Landscapes of Power: From Detroit to Disney World*. Berkeley and Los Angeles: University of California Press, 1991.

———. "Changing Landscapes of Power: Opulence and the Urge for Authenticity." *International Journal of Urban and Regional Research* 33, no. 2 (2009): 548–9.

———. *Naked City: The Death and Life of Authentic Urban Places*. New York: Oxford University Press, 2010.

THE MACAT LIBRARY
BY DISCIPLINE

AFRICANA STUDIES

Chinua Achebe's *An Image of Africa: Racism in Conrad's Heart of Darkness*
W. E. B. Du Bois's *The Souls of Black Folk*
Zora Neale Huston's *Characteristics of Negro Expression*
Martin Luther King Jr's *Why We Can't Wait*
Toni Morrison's *Playing in the Dark: Whiteness in the American Literary Imagination*

ANTHROPOLOGY

Arjun Appadurai's *Modernity at Large: Cultural Dimensions of Globalisation*
Philippe Ariès's *Centuries of Childhood*
Franz Boas's *Race, Language and Culture*
Kim Chan & Renée Mauborgne's *Blue Ocean Strategy*
Jared Diamond's *Guns, Germs & Steel: the Fate of Human Societies*
Jared Diamond's *Collapse: How Societies Choose to Fail or Survive*
E. E. Evans-Pritchard's *Witchcraft, Oracles and Magic Among the Azande*
James Ferguson's *The Anti-Politics Machine*
Clifford Geertz's *The Interpretation of Cultures*
David Graeber's *Debt: the First 5000 Years*
Karen Ho's *Liquidated: An Ethnography of Wall Street*
Geert Hofstede's *Culture's Consequences: Comparing Values, Behaviors, Institutes and Organizations across Nations*
Claude Lévi-Strauss's *Structural Anthropology*
Jay Macleod's *Ain't No Makin' It: Aspirations and Attainment in a Low-Income Neighborhood*
Saba Mahmood's *The Politics of Piety: The Islamic Revival and the Feminist Subject*
Marcel Mauss's *The Gift*

BUSINESS

Jean Lave & Etienne Wenger's *Situated Learning*
Theodore Levitt's *Marketing Myopia*
Burton G. Malkiel's *A Random Walk Down Wall Street*
Douglas McGregor's *The Human Side of Enterprise*
Michael Porter's *Competitive Strategy: Creating and Sustaining Superior Performance*
John Kotter's *Leading Change*
C. K. Prahalad & Gary Hamel's *The Core Competence of the Corporation*

CRIMINOLOGY

Michelle Alexander's *The New Jim Crow: Mass Incarceration in the Age of Colorblindness*
Michael R. Gottfredson & Travis Hirschi's *A General Theory of Crime*
Richard Herrnstein & Charles A. Murray's *The Bell Curve: Intelligence and Class Structure in American Life*
Elizabeth Loftus's *Eyewitness Testimony*
Jay Macleod's *Ain't No Makin' It: Aspirations and Attainment in a Low-Income Neighborhood*
Philip Zimbardo's *The Lucifer Effect*

ECONOMICS

Janet Abu-Lughod's *Before European Hegemony*
Ha-Joon Chang's *Kicking Away the Ladder*
David Brion Davis's *The Problem of Slavery in the Age of Revolution*
Milton Friedman's *The Role of Monetary Policy*
Milton Friedman's *Capitalism and Freedom*
David Graeber's *Debt: the First 5000 Years*
Friedrich Hayek's *The Road to Serfdom*
Karen Ho's *Liquidated: An Ethnography of Wall Street*

John Maynard Keynes's *The General Theory of Employment, Interest and Money*
Charles P. Kindleberger's *Manias, Panics and Crashes*
Robert Lucas's *Why Doesn't Capital Flow from Rich to Poor Countries?*
Burton G. Malkiel's *A Random Walk Down Wall Street*
Thomas Robert Malthus's *An Essay on the Principle of Population*
Karl Marx's *Capital*
Thomas Piketty's *Capital in the Twenty-First Century*
Amartya Sen's *Development as Freedom*
Adam Smith's *The Wealth of Nations*
Nassim Nicholas Taleb's *The Black Swan: The Impact of the Highly Improbable*
Amos Tversky's & Daniel Kahneman's *Judgment under Uncertainty: Heuristics and Biases*
Mahbub Ul Haq's *Reflections on Human Development*
Max Weber's *The Protestant Ethic and the Spirit of Capitalism*

FEMINISM AND GENDER STUDIES

Judith Butler's *Gender Trouble*
Simone De Beauvoir's *The Second Sex*
Michel Foucault's *History of Sexuality*
Betty Friedan's *The Feminine Mystique*
Saba Mahmood's *The Politics of Piety: The Islamic Revival and the Feminist Subject*
Joan Wallach Scott's *Gender and the Politics of History*
Mary Wollstonecraft's *A Vindication of the Rights of Woman*
Virginia Woolf's *A Room of One's Own*

GEOGRAPHY

The Brundtland Report's *Our Common Future*
Rachel Carson's *Silent Spring*
Charles Darwin's *On the Origin of Species*
James Ferguson's *The Anti-Politics Machine*
Jane Jacobs's *The Death and Life of Great American Cities*
James Lovelock's *Gaia: A New Look at Life on Earth*
Amartya Sen's *Development as Freedom*
Mathis Wackernagel & William Rees's *Our Ecological Footprint*

HISTORY

Janet Abu-Lughod's *Before European Hegemony*
Benedict Anderson's *Imagined Communities*
Bernard Bailyn's *The Ideological Origins of the American Revolution*
Hanna Batatu's *The Old Social Classes And The Revolutionary Movements Of Iraq*
Christopher Browning's *Ordinary Men: Reserve Police Batallion 101 and the Final Solution in Poland*
Edmund Burke's *Reflections on the Revolution in France*
William Cronon's *Nature's Metropolis: Chicago And The Great West*
Alfred W. Crosby's *The Columbian Exchange*
Hamid Dabashi's *Iran: A People Interrupted*
David Brion Davis's *The Problem of Slavery in the Age of Revolution*
Nathalie Zemon Davis's *The Return of Martin Guerre*
Jared Diamond's *Guns, Germs & Steel: the Fate of Human Societies*
Frank Dikotter's *Mao's Great Famine*
John W Dower's *War Without Mercy: Race And Power In The Pacific War*
W. E. B. Du Bois's *The Souls of Black Folk*
Richard J. Evans's *In Defence of History*
Lucien Febvre's *The Problem of Unbelief in the 16th Century*
Sheila Fitzpatrick's *Everyday Stalinism*

The Macat Library By Discipline

Eric Foner's *Reconstruction: America's Unfinished Revolution, 1863-1877*
Michel Foucault's *Discipline and Punish*
Michel Foucault's *History of Sexuality*
Francis Fukuyama's *The End of History and the Last Man*
John Lewis Gaddis's *We Now Know: Rethinking Cold War History*
Ernest Gellner's *Nations and Nationalism*
Eugene Genovese's *Roll, Jordan, Roll: The World the Slaves Made*
Carlo Ginzburg's *The Night Battles*
Daniel Goldhagen's *Hitler's Willing Executioners*
Jack Goldstone's *Revolution and Rebellion in the Early Modern World*
Antonio Gramsci's *The Prison Notebooks*
Alexander Hamilton, John Jay & James Madison's *The Federalist Papers*
Christopher Hill's *The World Turned Upside Down*
Carole Hillenbrand's *The Crusades: Islamic Perspectives*
Thomas Hobbes's *Leviathan*
Eric Hobsbawm's *The Age Of Revolution*
John A. Hobson's *Imperialism: A Study*
Albert Hourani's *History of the Arab Peoples*
Samuel P. Huntington's *The Clash of Civilizations and the Remaking of World Order*
C. L. R. James's *The Black Jacobins*
Tony Judt's *Postwar: A History of Europe Since 1945*
Ernst Kantorowicz's *The King's Two Bodies: A Study in Medieval Political Theology*
Paul Kennedy's *The Rise and Fall of the Great Powers*
Ian Kershaw's *The "Hitler Myth": Image and Reality in the Third Reich*
John Maynard Keynes's *The General Theory of Employment, Interest and Money*
Charles P. Kindleberger's *Manias, Panics and Crashes*
Martin Luther King Jr's *Why We Can't Wait*
Henry Kissinger's *World Order: Reflections on the Character of Nations and the Course of History*
Thomas Kuhn's *The Structure of Scientific Revolutions*
Georges Lefebvre's *The Coming of the French Revolution*
John Locke's *Two Treatises of Government*
Niccolò Machiavelli's *The Prince*
Thomas Robert Malthus's *An Essay on the Principle of Population*
Mahmood Mamdani's *Citizen and Subject: Contemporary Africa And The Legacy Of Late Colonialism*
Karl Marx's *Capital*
Stanley Milgram's *Obedience to Authority*
John Stuart Mill's *On Liberty*
Thomas Paine's *Common Sense*
Thomas Paine's *Rights of Man*
Geoffrey Parker's *Global Crisis: War, Climate Change and Catastrophe in the Seventeenth Century*
Jonathan Riley-Smith's *The First Crusade and the Idea of Crusading*
Jean-Jacques Rousseau's *The Social Contract*
Joan Wallach Scott's *Gender and the Politics of History*
Theda Skocpol's *States and Social Revolutions*
Adam Smith's *The Wealth of Nations*
Timothy Snyder's *Bloodlands: Europe Between Hitler and Stalin*
Sun Tzu's *The Art of War*
Keith Thomas's *Religion and the Decline of Magic*
Thucydides's *The History of the Peloponnesian War*
Frederick Jackson Turner's *The Significance of the Frontier in American History*
Odd Arne Westad's *The Global Cold War: Third World Interventions And The Making Of Our Times*

LITERATURE

Chinua Achebe's *An Image of Africa: Racism in Conrad's Heart of Darkness*
Roland Barthes's *Mythologies*
Homi K. Bhabha's *The Location of Culture*
Judith Butler's *Gender Trouble*
Simone De Beauvoir's *The Second Sex*
Ferdinand De Saussure's *Course in General Linguistics*
T. S. Eliot's *The Sacred Wood: Essays on Poetry and Criticism*
Zora Neale Huston's *Characteristics of Negro Expression*
Toni Morrison's *Playing in the Dark: Whiteness in the American Literary Imagination*
Edward Said's *Orientalism*
Gayatri Chakravorty Spivak's *Can the Subaltern Speak?*
Mary Wollstonecraft's *A Vindication of the Rights of Women*
Virginia Woolf's *A Room of One's Own*

PHILOSOPHY

Elizabeth Anscombe's *Modern Moral Philosophy*
Hannah Arendt's *The Human Condition*
Aristotle's *Metaphysics*
Aristotle's *Nicomachean Ethics*
Edmund Gettier's *Is Justified True Belief Knowledge?*
Georg Wilhelm Friedrich Hegel's *Phenomenology of Spirit*
David Hume's *Dialogues Concerning Natural Religion*
David Hume's *The Enquiry for Human Understanding*
Immanuel Kant's *Religion within the Boundaries of Mere Reason*
Immanuel Kant's *Critique of Pure Reason*
Søren Kierkegaard's *The Sickness Unto Death*
Søren Kierkegaard's *Fear and Trembling*
C. S. Lewis's *The Abolition of Man*
Alasdair MacIntyre's *After Virtue*
Marcus Aurelius's *Meditations*
Friedrich Nietzsche's *On the Genealogy of Morality*
Friedrich Nietzsche's *Beyond Good and Evil*
Plato's *Republic*
Plato's *Symposium*
Jean-Jacques Rousseau's *The Social Contract*
Gilbert Ryle's *The Concept of Mind*
Baruch Spinoza's *Ethics*
Sun Tzu's *The Art of War*
Ludwig Wittgenstein's *Philosophical Investigations*

POLITICS

Benedict Anderson's *Imagined Communities*
Aristotle's *Politics*
Bernard Bailyn's *The Ideological Origins of the American Revolution*
Edmund Burke's *Reflections on the Revolution in France*
John C. Calhoun's *A Disquisition on Government*
Ha-Joon Chang's *Kicking Away the Ladder*
Hamid Dabashi's *Iran: A People Interrupted*
Hamid Dabashi's *Theology of Discontent: The Ideological Foundation of the Islamic Revolution in Iran*
Robert Dahl's *Democracy and its Critics*
Robert Dahl's *Who Governs?*
David Brion Davis's *The Problem of Slavery in the Age of Revolution*

The Macat Library By Discipline

Alexis De Tocqueville's *Democracy in America*
James Ferguson's *The Anti-Politics Machine*
Frank Dikotter's *Mao's Great Famine*
Sheila Fitzpatrick's *Everyday Stalinism*
Eric Foner's *Reconstruction: America's Unfinished Revolution, 1863-1877*
Milton Friedman's *Capitalism and Freedom*
Francis Fukuyama's *The End of History and the Last Man*
John Lewis Gaddis's *We Now Know: Rethinking Cold War History*
Ernest Gellner's *Nations and Nationalism*
David Graeber's *Debt: the First 5000 Years*
Antonio Gramsci's *The Prison Notebooks*
Alexander Hamilton, John Jay & James Madison's *The Federalist Papers*
Friedrich Hayek's *The Road to Serfdom*
Christopher Hill's *The World Turned Upside Down*
Thomas Hobbes's *Leviathan*
John A. Hobson's *Imperialism: A Study*
Samuel P. Huntington's *The Clash of Civilizations and the Remaking of World Order*
Tony Judt's *Postwar: A History of Europe Since 1945*
David C. Kang's *China Rising: Peace, Power and Order in East Asia*
Paul Kennedy's *The Rise and Fall of Great Powers*
Robert Keohane's *After Hegemony*
Martin Luther King Jr.'s *Why We Can't Wait*
Henry Kissinger's *World Order: Reflections on the Character of Nations and the Course of History*
John Locke's *Two Treatises of Government*
Niccolò Machiavelli's *The Prince*
Thomas Robert Malthus's *An Essay on the Principle of Population*
Mahmood Mamdani's *Citizen and Subject: Contemporary Africa And The Legacy Of Late Colonialism*
Karl Marx's *Capital*
John Stuart Mill's *On Liberty*
John Stuart Mill's *Utilitarianism*
Hans Morgenthau's *Politics Among Nations*
Thomas Paine's *Common Sense*
Thomas Paine's *Rights of Man*
Thomas Piketty's *Capital in the Twenty-First Century*
Robert D. Putman's *Bowling Alone*
John Rawls's *Theory of Justice*
Jean-Jacques Rousseau's *The Social Contract*
Theda Skocpol's *States and Social Revolutions*
Adam Smith's *The Wealth of Nations*
Sun Tzu's *The Art of War*
Henry David Thoreau's *Civil Disobedience*
Thucydides's *The History of the Peloponnesian War*
Kenneth Waltz's *Theory of International Politics*
Max Weber's *Politics as a Vocation*
Odd Arne Westad's *The Global Cold War: Third World Interventions And The Making Of Our Times*

POSTCOLONIAL STUDIES

Roland Barthes's *Mythologies*
Frantz Fanon's *Black Skin, White Masks*
Homi K. Bhabha's *The Location of Culture*
Gustavo Gutiérrez's *A Theology of Liberation*
Edward Said's *Orientalism*
Gayatri Chakravorty Spivak's *Can the Subaltern Speak?*

PSYCHOLOGY

Gordon Allport's *The Nature of Prejudice*
Alan Baddeley & Graham Hitch's *Aggression: A Social Learning Analysis*
Albert Bandura's *Aggression: A Social Learning Analysis*
Leon Festinger's *A Theory of Cognitive Dissonance*
Sigmund Freud's *The Interpretation of Dreams*
Betty Friedan's *The Feminine Mystique*
Michael R. Gottfredson & Travis Hirschi's *A General Theory of Crime*
Eric Hoffer's *The True Believer: Thoughts on the Nature of Mass Movements*
William James's *Principles of Psychology*
Elizabeth Loftus's *Eyewitness Testimony*
A. H. Maslow's *A Theory of Human Motivation*
Stanley Milgram's *Obedience to Authority*
Steven Pinker's *The Better Angels of Our Nature*
Oliver Sacks's *The Man Who Mistook His Wife For a Hat*
Richard Thaler & Cass Sunstein's *Nudge: Improving Decisions About Health, Wealth and Happiness*
Amos Tversky's *Judgment under Uncertainty: Heuristics and Biases*
Philip Zimbardo's *The Lucifer Effect*

SCIENCE

Rachel Carson's *Silent Spring*
William Cronon's *Nature's Metropolis: Chicago And The Great West*
Alfred W. Crosby's *The Columbian Exchange*
Charles Darwin's *On the Origin of Species*
Richard Dawkin's *The Selfish Gene*
Thomas Kuhn's *The Structure of Scientific Revolutions*
Geoffrey Parker's *Global Crisis: War, Climate Change and Catastrophe in the Seventeenth Century*
Mathis Wackernagel & William Rees's *Our Ecological Footprint*

SOCIOLOGY

Michelle Alexander's *The New Jim Crow: Mass Incarceration in the Age of Colorblindness*
Gordon Allport's *The Nature of Prejudice*
Albert Bandura's *Aggression: A Social Learning Analysis*
Hanna Batatu's *The Old Social Classes And The Revolutionary Movements Of Iraq*
Ha-Joon Chang's *Kicking Away the Ladder*
W. E. B. Du Bois's *The Souls of Black Folk*
Émile Durkheim's *On Suicide*
Frantz Fanon's *Black Skin, White Masks*
Frantz Fanon's *The Wretched of the Earth*
Eric Foner's *Reconstruction: America's Unfinished Revolution, 1863-1877*
Eugene Genovese's *Roll, Jordan, Roll: The World the Slaves Made*
Jack Goldstone's *Revolution and Rebellion in the Early Modern World*
Antonio Gramsci's *The Prison Notebooks*
Richard Herrnstein & Charles A Murray's *The Bell Curve: Intelligence and Class Structure in American Life*
Eric Hoffer's *The True Believer: Thoughts on the Nature of Mass Movements*
Jane Jacobs's *The Death and Life of Great American Cities*
Robert Lucas's *Why Doesn't Capital Flow from Rich to Poor Countries?*
Jay Macleod's *Ain't No Makin' It: Aspirations and Attainment in a Low Income Neighborhood*
Elaine May's *Homeward Bound: American Families in the Cold War Era*
Douglas McGregor's *The Human Side of Enterprise*
C. Wright Mills's *The Sociological Imagination*

Thomas Piketty's *Capital in the Twenty-First Century*
Robert D. Putman's *Bowling Alone*
David Riesman's *The Lonely Crowd: A Study of the Changing American Character*
Edward Said's *Orientalism*
Joan Wallach Scott's *Gender and the Politics of History*
Theda Skocpol's *States and Social Revolutions*
Max Weber's *The Protestant Ethic and the Spirit of Capitalism*

THEOLOGY

Augustine's *Confessions*
Benedict's *Rule of St Benedict*
Gustavo Gutiérrez's *A Theology of Liberation*
Carole Hillenbrand's *The Crusades: Islamic Perspectives*
David Hume's *Dialogues Concerning Natural Religion*
Immanuel Kant's *Religion within the Boundaries of Mere Reason*
Ernst Kantorowicz's *The King's Two Bodies: A Study in Medieval Political Theology*
Søren Kierkegaard's *The Sickness Unto Death*
C. S. Lewis's *The Abolition of Man*
Saba Mahmood's *The Politics of Piety: The Islamic Revival and the Feminist Subject*
Baruch Spinoza's *Ethics*
Keith Thomas's *Religion and the Decline of Magic*

COMING SOON

Chris Argyris's *The Individual and the Organisation*
Seyla Benhabib's *The Rights of Others*
Walter Benjamin's *The Work Of Art in the Age of Mechanical Reproduction*
John Berger's *Ways of Seeing*
Pierre Bourdieu's *Outline of a Theory of Practice*
Mary Douglas's *Purity and Danger*
Roland Dworkin's *Taking Rights Seriously*
James G. March's *Exploration and Exploitation in Organisational Learning*
Ikujiro Nonaka's *A Dynamic Theory of Organizational Knowledge Creation*
Griselda Pollock's *Vision and Difference*
Amartya Sen's *Inequality Re-Examined*
Susan Sontag's *On Photography*
Yasser Tabbaa's *The Transformation of Islamic Art*
Ludwig von Mises's *Theory of Money and Credit*

Printed in the United States
by Baker & Taylor Publisher Services